Contents

GOOGLE DOCS
MADE EASY

Online Collaboration For Everyone

By James Bernstein

Introduction

With more and more of us working from home and taking our classes in our living rooms, there becomes more of a need to be able to do your work online so it can be shared with your coworkers, teachers or fellow students. Sure you can email your documents back and forth every time you need to update something but that can become tedious and it's also a great way for information to get lost within your inbox since you might not know which is the most current version of your document.

Google has been one of the pioneers of online collaboration since online collaboration was a thing. You might have thought Google was just a search engine that most people used to find information online, but they have an entire suite of office productivity apps that anyone with a Google account can use for free.

If you are familiar with Microsoft Office and all of the software that comes with the productivity suite then you might want to know that Google offers similar apps that can do just about everything that Office can do. I call them apps rather than software because software is more of a term for something you install on your computer where an app is more of something you can use without installing it for the most part and also use it online with many different devices.

Google Docs is Google's word processing app and is very similar to Microsoft Word and it will get the job done for most of us. Sure Word has many more advanced features but if you don't need all of that super geeky stuff then Docs will work just fine for you and best of all, it's free to use.

The goal of this book is to get you up and running with Google Docs and show you how to make great looking documents and also how to collaborate with other people using your online documents. I will also go over other advanced features for those who wish to get the most out of this powerful app. So on that note... I mean document, let's get started!

Chapter 1 – Introducing Google Docs

Google Docs has been around since 2006 so there is a good chance that you have at least heard of it even if you have not used it. There is also a good chance that you have opened a Google Doc that someone else might have sent you a link to and not even realized it was a Google Doc since many people like to share their documents using this format.

If you have ever used a program like Microsoft Word, Apple Pages, LibreOffice Writer, WordPerfect or any other word processing type software then using Google Docs should be pretty easy to get used to since many of these programs work in a very similar way.

Figure 1.1 shows a document open within Google Docs and as you can see it most likely looks similar to whatever word processing program you are using now or have used in the past. You have the body of your document with images in the middle and menu items and a toolbar on the top of the page.

The main thing you will need to get used to when using Docs is knowing where to find the tools and features you need to accomplish the task at hand. You will also need to know what features Docs has so you will even know if you are able to accomplish that particular task.

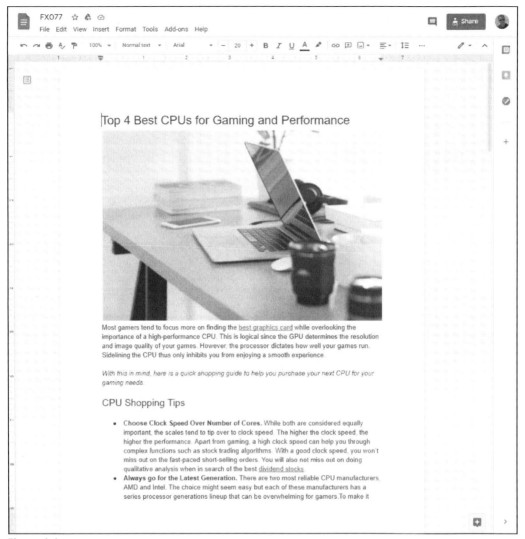

Figure 1.1

Signing Up For a Google Account

In order to use Docs, you will need to have a Google account to log in with. If you have a Gmail account then you already have a Google account, and you can use that account for Docs. Most people use the free Google accounts even though there are subscription based accounts that give you additional features but for the home or small business user, the free account works just fine.

If you are planning on just using a free account to login and don't have one then it's very easy to sign up for one. To begin, simply open your web browser and navigate to **https://accounts.google.com/** and you will be prompted to enter your account details such as name, desired email address and a password to go along with your new account.

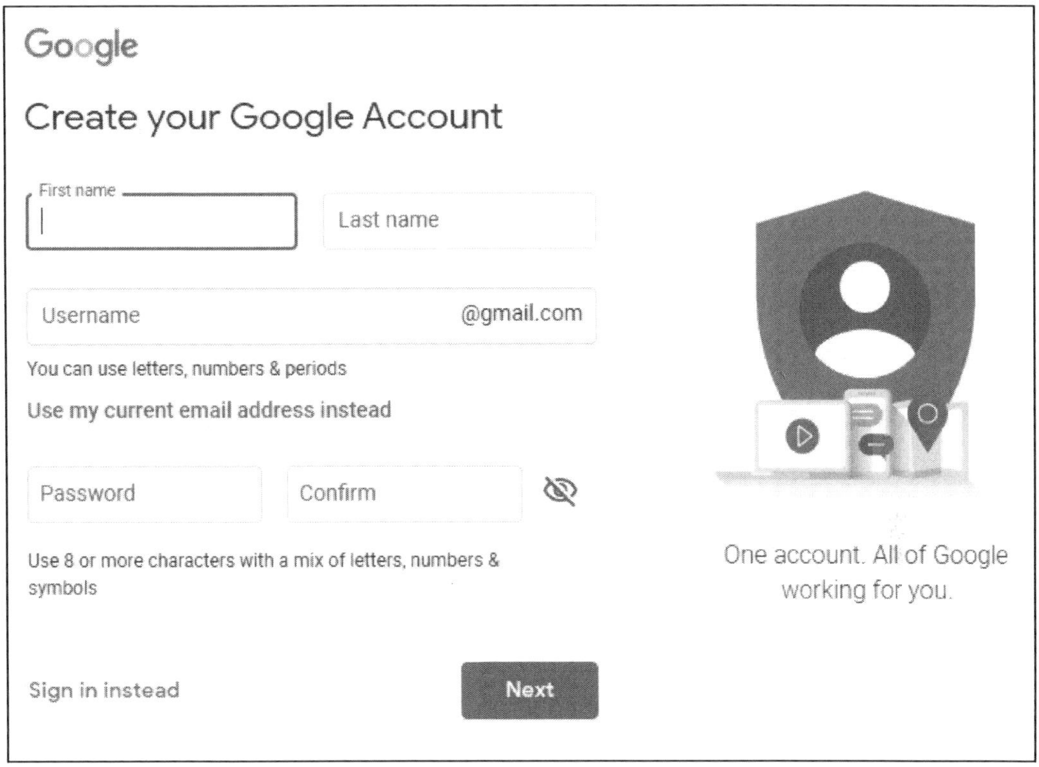

Figure 1.2

Simply enter your first and last name and choose a username, which will also be used for your Gmail email account ending in *@gmail.com*. If the username has already been taken, then you will be prompted to enter a new one. Notice that there is an option that says *Use my current email address instead*. This can be used if you do not want a Gmail email address, but still want to create a Google account with your current email address.

Then you will need to come up with a password that has 8 or more characters and uses letters, numbers, and symbols (such as **!** or **#** for example) and click on *Next*.

After that, you will need to enter your phone number so Google can verify it is really you. It will send you a six digit number via text message that you will have to enter in the next step. Doing this will also tie your phone number to your Google account, which comes in handy for things like password recovery if you forget your password. If you don't have a smartphone you can have Google call you with the code instead of texting it.

Next, you enter a recovery email address (which can also be used for password recovery), as well as your birth date information. The birth date information is used because some Google services have age requirements. The gender information it asks for is optional and is not shown to other Google users. You can also edit your Google account later if you wish to change or add anything.

If you *don't* want your number to be used at all, simply click on *Skip,* and you will be brought to the *Privacy and Terms* agreement, which you can read if you like. To continue, you will need to click on the *I agree* button. Finally, after clicking on *I agree,* your account will be created, and you will be logged in automatically. If you are on the Google home page, then you will see your first initial up in the right hand corner. You can go into your settings and edit your profile and add a picture if you like.

Accessing Google Docs
Once you have your Google account configured and you are logged in then it's very easy to get to Google Docs and there are a couple of ways to do so. If you are on the Google home page in your web browser then you will see what is known as the "Google waffle" icon at the top right of the screen next to your initials as seen in figure 1.3.

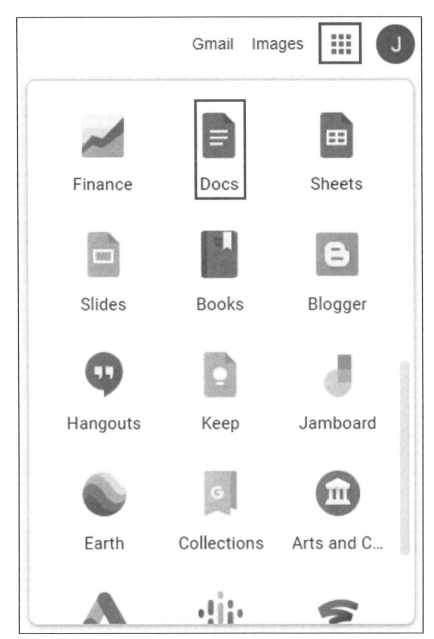

Figure 1.3

When you click on this icon you will be shown the Google Apps that are available to use with your account. You can then scroll down until you find Google Docs and click on it to open the app. You can also drag the Docs icon to the top of the list if you plan on using it often.

 If you are interested in learning more about the other Google Apps that are available to you then check out my book titled **Google Apps Made Easy**.
https://www.amazon.com/dp/1798114992

Another way to access Google Docs is by going directly to the Docs website from your web browser. All you need to do is type in **docs.google.com** in the address bar of your browser and you will be taken to the Docs website and if you are logged into your Google account then you will see all of your documents right when you are taken there.

If you use bookmarks\favorites in your browser then you can simply add the Docs site to your bookmarks or even on your quick access bookmark bar within your browser for even faster access.

You can even do a search for *Google Docs* from the search box from your browser using your favorite search engine and it should be the first choice in the search results. If you plan on using a lot of the Google Apps then you might want to think about using the Chrome web browser as well for the best results since that is made by Google as well. You can download it for free from the Google website.

Docs Interface
Even though I will be going into the Docs interface in greater detail as I go through this book, I wanted to take a moment to give you a brief overview of the layout of the Docs app so things will make a little more sense as we go along.

If you take a look back at figure 1.1 you will see how the main document area where you type takes up most of the screen and then you have other items off to the side where you go to do things such as format text, insert pictures, print your document and so on.

Figure 1.4 shows the top of the Docs interface where you will find the title of your document, the menu items which contain various tools and settings and also the toolbar items which contain many of the same tools and settings you will find in the menu item area.

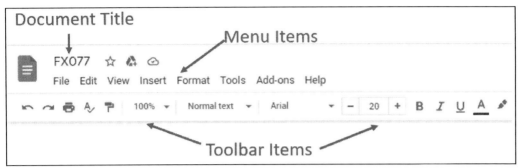

Figure 1.4

Figure 1.5 shows the upper right corner of the Docs interface where you will find your sharing\collaboration options, comment history, editing modes, apps and add-ons and also Google account\profile options.

I will be going over all of these menus and settings throughout the book but you might want to play around with these items so you will have an idea of what is located where because that will make things easier to follow along with.

Figure 1.5

You will spend most of your time in the body (on the page) of the Docs interface as you type and insert things such as pictures, tables, columns and so on throughout your document. Most word processor users probably only use about 10% of the features that their software offers so don't feel bad if you find that many of these items seem like something you will never use, because you just might not!

Saving Documents

One last thing I wanted to quickly go over in this chapter is the process of saving your documents. You might have noticed that there is no *Save* option when browsing through the menu items, especially the *File* menu.

Docs doesn't work like the typical word processing software that you would install on your computer such as Word or Pages. With these types of programs, you save your documents at locations such as your hard drive, USB drive or network drive, and then when you need to open that document, it will look exactly the same as the last time you saved it.

The way Docs saves your documents is that every time you make a change even if it's as small as adding a period to the end of a sentence. So think of Docs as saving your document in real time rather than you having to manually save it as you think to do so. Many programs such as Microsoft Word (and other Office software) will have auto save options which will save a copy of your file at set intervals in case your computer crashes and you need to recover your document. Just keep in mind that your document will only be as current as your last auto save.

If you are a Microsoft Office use and would like to increase your Office skill levels and learn more about how the software works then check out my book titled **Office Made Easy**. https://www.amazon.com/dp/1729013732

You might be wondering where Docs saves your documents to if you are not manually saving them yourself. And if so, that's a very good question! Docs will automatically save your documents to your *Google Drive* which is your online cloud storage account that comes free with your Google account. You can access your Drive files and folders from the Google waffle item the same way you access Docs. Or you can do a search for Google Drive itself.

Figure 1.6 shows my Drive online storage account for one of my Google accounts (and yes you can have more than one). Within Drive you can create folders to organize your files and even mark certain files as favorites by using the *Starred* feature.

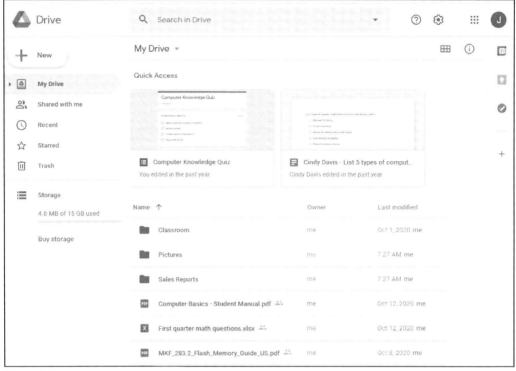

Figure 1.6

Google Drive is not just for Docs files but rather you can store any type of file you like here such as pictures, videos, music, spreadsheets and so on. The files you store here do not have to be from a Google app either and you can save things like your Microsoft Office files here as well etc.

I will have an entire chapter devoted to Google Drive so don't worry if it's a little confusing for now. You might want to play around in your own Drive before getting to the chapter on Drive in the book so things will make a little more sense while you are reading the information.

Chapter 2 - Toolbar and Menu Items

To get the most of Docs you will need to be able to do things such as format your document to make it more presentable, print your document if needed, share your documents with others, check for spelling and grammar errors and so on. To be able to perform these tasks, you will need to know where to find them and where you will find these tools is with the toolbar and menu items.

In this chapter, I will be going over all of the toolbar buttons and menu items so you have an idea about what each one does and also so you will know where to find them. This might not be the most exciting chapter, but it will have some very useful information so please try and stay awake!

Toolbar Items
Since there are many buttons and tools on the Docs toolbar, I will break them down into sections and discuss them one section at a time. I will be going into more detail about many of these tools throughout the book but for now I will give you an overview of what each one is used for.

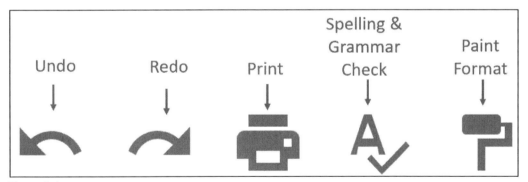

Figure 2.1

- **Undo** – Use this to undo the last change you made to your document. For example, if you deleted a paragraph and then decided you didn't want to do that, you can click on the Undo button to have it brought back. You can use the Undo feature many times to undo multiple changes that you have made.

- **Redo** – If you use the Undo option to undo a change but then decide that you want to redo the change then you would use this button.

- **Print** – This will bring up the print dialog box where you can choose your printer and printing options. More on this in Chapter 3.

- **Spelling & Grammar Check** – Docs has its own built in spelling and grammar checker that you can use to proofread your document. I will be discussing how to use this feature in Chapter 4.

- **Paint Format** – The Paint format button is used to apply formatting from one part of your document to another so things like the font and colors etc. match rather than having to try and match everything manually. I will be going into more detail on this tool in Chapter 4.

Figure 2.2

- **Zoom** – This is used to change how large the page\text shows on your screen. It does not affect how large the text is on the document or what size it will print.

- **Text Style** – Text styles include normal text that you would use for the body of your document as well as title and heading text that you would use for things such as outlines and a table of contents or to simply break up your document into sections.

- **Font** – Here is where you can change the typestyle that is used in your document. I will be showing you how to format your text and even how to add additional fonts in Chapter 4.

- **Font Size** – If you need to adjust the size of your text then you can simply highlight the text you want to change and then increase or decrease its size.

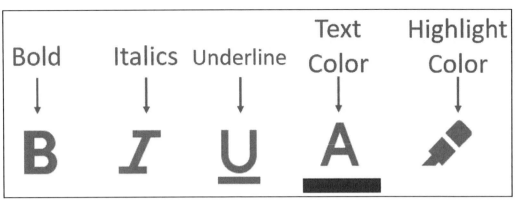

Figure 2.3

- **Bold** – Use this to make your text **bold**.

- **Italics** – Use this to *italicize* your text.

- **Underline** – Use this to <u>underline</u> your text.

- **Text Color** – Use this to change the color of your text.

- **Highlight Color** – Docs has a highlighter tool that works like an actual highlighter marker you would use to highlight the text on your paper. You can change the color of the highlight using this option.

Choose Clock Speed Over Number of Cores. While both are considered equally important, the scales tend to tip over to clock speed. The higher the clock speed, the higher the performance. Apart from gaming, a high clock speed can help you through complex functions such as stock trading algorithms. With a good clock speed, you won't miss out on the fast-paced short-selling orders. You will also not miss out on doing qualitative analysis when in search of the best dividend stocks.

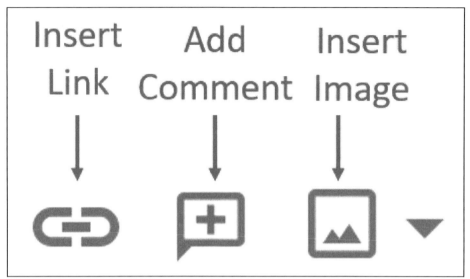

Figure 2.4

- **Insert Link** – You can insert various types of links into your documents such as links to websites, links to other documents and links to other sections of your current document. More about links in Chapters 3 and 5.

- **Add Comment** – Comments are used for collaboration purposes where you would like to make a note for others to see so they can do things such as approve a change or make their own additions to your document. I will be discussing comments in Chapter 5.

- **Insert Image** – Docs will let you insert images into your document from sources such as your local computer\mobile device, your Drive folders, a website or even directly from your camera.

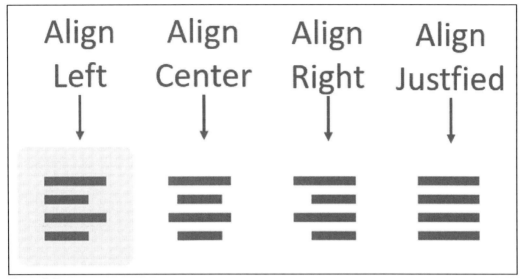

Figure 2.5

- **Align Left** – By default, the text in your paragraphs will be left aligned like shown in the example below.

> Most gamers tend to focus more on finding the best graphics card while overlooking the importance of a high-performance CPU. This is logical since the GPU determines the resolution and image quality of your games. However, the processor dictates how well your games run. Sidelining the CPU thus only inhibits you from enjoying a smooth experience.

- **Align Center** – If you want your paragraph text to be centered then use the align center option.

> Most gamers tend to focus more on finding the best graphics card while overlooking the importance of a high-performance CPU. This is logical since the GPU determines the resolution and image quality of your games. However, the processor dictates how well your games run. Sidelining the CPU thus only inhibits you from enjoying a smooth experience.

- **Align Right** – The align right option will align your text to the right hand side of the page.

> Most gamers tend to focus more on finding the best graphics card while overlooking the importance of a high-performance CPU. This is logical since the GPU determines the resolution and image quality of your games. However, the processor dictates how well your games run. Sidelining the CPU thus only inhibits you from enjoying a smooth experience.

- **Align Justified** – This option will align your text to the left and right side of the page by slightly spacing out the words in your paragraphs to make them fit.

Most gamers tend to focus more on finding the best graphics card while overlooking the importance of a high-performance CPU. This is logical since the GPU determines the resolution and image quality of your games. However, the processor dictates how well your games run. Sidelining the CPU thus only inhibits you from enjoying a smooth experience.

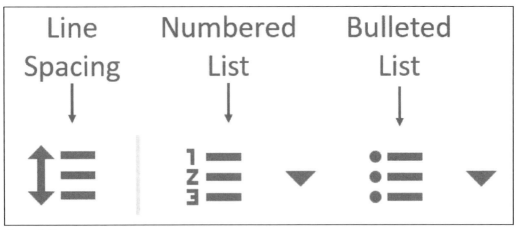

Figure 2.6

- **Line Spacing** – Line spacing is used to adjust how much space you have between lines of text in your document. The sample below shows how the spacing looks when changed from the default setting of 1.15 to double spacing.

Most gamers tend to focus more on finding the best graphics card while overlooking the

importance of a high-performance CPU. This is logical since the GPU determines the resolution

and image quality of your games. However, the processor dictates how well your games run.

Sidelining the CPU thus only inhibits you from enjoying a smooth experience.

- **Numbered List** – Lists come in handy to help you organize your content so it's easier to understand. You can use a numbered list to organize information in a step by step list as seen below. I will be going over lists in more detail in Chapter 4.

How to be a Google Docs expert
1. Buy book
2. Read book
3. Become a Google Docs expert

- **Bulleted List** – These are similar to numbered lists but use bullet points rather than numbers.

How to be a Google Docs expert
- Buy book
- Read book
- Become a Google Docs expert

Figure 2.7

- **Decrease and Increase Indent** – Indents are used to offset a sentence or paragraph like you would sometimes see at the beginning of a chapter. The sample text below shows indented text on the middle paragraph.

> This Intel Core i9 processor is the 9th Generation of the Intel line up. The CPU rocks a boost clock speed of 5GHz making it a powerhouse for gamers and busy creatives alike.
>
> > Adding to its high performance are solid eight 8 cores and 16 threads, giving the i9 boost performance. Just in case that is not enough, you can overclock to squeeze out more performance from the processor.
>
> Unfortunately, the Core i9-9900k didn't upgrade from the 14-nanometre technology used in its predecessors. However, this still means that the processor gives you backward compatibility with old Z370 chipsets.

- **Clear Formatting** – If you have applied formatting to some text such as changing the color, font, line spacing etc. and want to change everything back to the default Doc settings then all you need to do is highlight the text you want to clear the formatting on and then click the Clear formatting button.

Menu Items

The next topic I will be discussing will be the menu items that you see at the top of the screen above the toolbar. As you can see there are eight menu items and they are named File, Edit, View, Insert, Format, Tools, Add-ons and Help. I will now go over the options in each one of these menu items.

 If you notice that something doesn't match up or is not located where it used to be that is most likely because Google thought it was a good idea to change things around. Many software developers do this to "improve" their apps but don't consider how it affects those of us who have to find where they moved these things to!

File menu

The File menu is probably the most uses of all the menus and here is what you will find on this menu item.

Share – Here is where you can go to share your document with other people either via a message sent to them or via a link that you can send to them. This will be discussed in more detail in Chapter 5.

New – This will open a new blank document or allow you to open a template.

Open – Here you can open an existing document that you saved on your Google Drive that was shared with you by someone else. You can also upload a file from your local computer to work on within Docs.

Make a copy – If you would like to create a copy of your document for someone else to work on so they don't work on your original document then you can simply make a copy and share the copy with them or store the copy on your Drive.

Email – You can email someone a copy of your file if you are into doing things the old fashioned way!

Download – This option lets you download a copy of your document to your computer's hard drive so you can have a copy that is local to your computer. You can save the file as another file type such as a Word or PDF document etc.

Make available offline – If for some reason you know you will be working in a location without an internet connection, you can make your document available to be worked on offline. When your document is available to work on offline, you will see a checkmark next to *Make available offline* indicating this. When you have an internet connection once again, you can make the document online by unchecking this menu item and all your changes will get synchronized back to the online version.

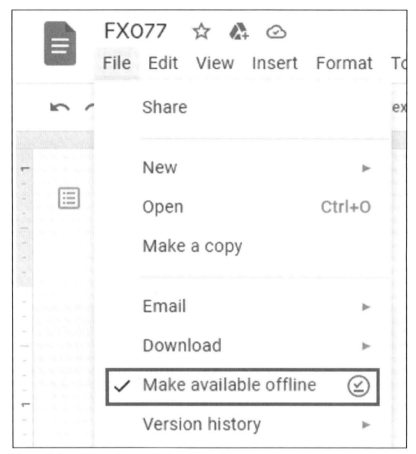

Figure 2.8

When working with a document offline, you will not have all of the same functionality available as you do when working online. For example, you won't be able to see edits online users are making to your documents and you can't share documents either. Once you make the document online again, you will be able to use all of the normal features that you are used to.

Version history – Docs keeps several older versions of your documents in case you need to go back to an earlier version. I will be going over how to use this feature in Chapter 7.

Rename – If you don't like the name of your document and want to give it a more appropriate name then you can do so from here.

Move – You can use the move option to move the location of your document to another folder within your Drive. You can even create a new folder right on the spot and move your document into that new folder.

Add shortcut to Drive – If you would like to create a shortcut to a document in another location within your Google Drive, you can do so from here. This gives you another way to access your document that might be faster than trying to find the actual file within your folders.

Move to trash – This will simply delete your document and put it in the trash can. Google Drive files that were in the trash would normally stay there until you emptied the trash but recently Google decided that files in the trash would automatically be deleted in 30 days so make sure you really mean to delete any files you put in the trash!

Publish to the web – If you would like to have your document available online in a web page format for others to view then you can do so from here. This will be discussed in further detail in Chapter 5.

Document details – This will give you some basic information about the document you are working on as seen below.

Document details   ✕

Location	🗀 My Drive
Owner	me
Modified	Oct 1, 2020 by me
Created	Oct 1, 2020

Figure 2.9

Language – If you need to change the language settings of your document then you can do so from here. Once you change the language it won't actually change the way your text is displayed but will rather do things such as change the spelling and grammar checker to match that language and also change the input method to match that language assuming it's a non-Latin language. In the example below it now gives me an option to choose an on screen keyboard based on the language I have selected.

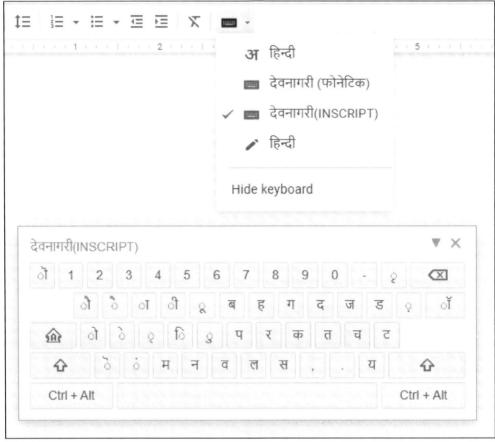

Figure 2.10

Page setup – Here is where you would go to change things such as the page size, orientation, margins and so on. I will be discussing these settings in more detail in Chapter 4.

Print – This will bring up the print dialog box where you can choose your printer and printing options. More on this in Chapter 3.

Edit Menu

Most of the items from this menu you should be familiar with if you have used any other type of word processing software.

Undo and Redo – I discussed these earlier in the chapter. This is just another way to get to them.

Cut – If you would like to remove text from one area to be pasted into another area of your document you would cut the text first by highlighting it and clicking on the Cut option.

Copy – This is used to copy any text that you have selected so it can then be pasted into another area of your document.

Paste – Once you have cut or copied your text, you will put the cursor where you want to place the text and then use the Paste option.

Paste without formatting – Normally when you paste text from one area of your document to another, it will keep the formatting (font, text size, text color etc.) and apply it when you paste the text. If you would like to paste your text without keeping the formatting choices then use this option.

Delete – Clicking on Delete will delete any text or images etc. that you have selected within your document. If you delete something on accident just remember that you can use the Undo feature to bring it back!

Select all – If you need to select everything in your document then you can easily do so using this option.

Find and replace – This feature is not used as often as the others but comes in very handy. Let's say you had spelled a person's name as **Jon** throughout your document rather than **John**. Rather than spend a lot of time trying to find every instance of Jon in your document so you can change it to John, you can use the Find and replace option to do it for you automatically. As you can see in figure 2.11 that there are 9 instances of Jon and you can either go through them one at a time and replace the ones you want, or you can click on the *Replace all* button to have them all replaced in one click.

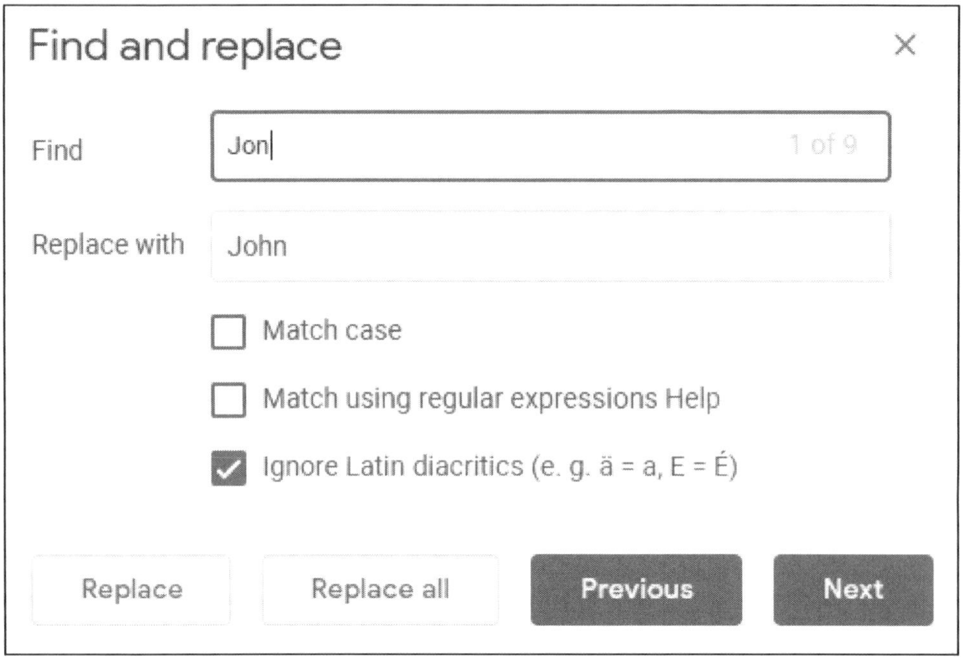

Find and replace ✕

Find | Jon| | 1 of 9

Replace with | John

☐ Match case

☐ Match using regular expressions Help

☑ Ignore Latin diacritics (e. g. ä = a, E = É)

Replace | Replace all | **Previous** | **Next**

Figure 2.11

View Menu

The View menu has options that well, change the way your document is viewed on the screen. There are not too many options here but it's still important to know what you can do from this menu.

Print layout – This is the default setting and will show you a view that matches how your document will look when printed. It shows each page separately and if you uncheck this option, your pages will only be separated by a dashed line.

Mode – There are three modes that you can use for your document and they are editing, suggesting and viewing with editing being the default modes. I will be going over each one of these modes in more detail in Chapter 5.

Show Ruler – The ruler is displayed at the top of the page and is used to view things such as your margin size or to get an idea of how large images are on your page. You can even use it to adjust margins and indents. I will be discussing this in Chapter 4.

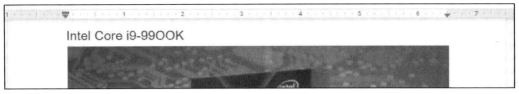

Figure 2.12

Show document outline – If you use text headings and titles in your document then you can use the outline view to see how your document is organized by clicking on the Show document outline button to the left of the page. More on document outlines in Chapter 4.

Figure 2.13

Show equation toolbar – If you are the type who likes to insert equations into your documents for maybe a math exam then you can check the setting for Show equation toolbar to have it show up in your Docs toolbar.

Figure 2.14

Show section breaks – If you like to use section breaks to break up your text and have it continued on a new page then you can use the Show section breaks option to have a dotted line be displayed where you inserted that break. Figures 2.15 and 2.16 shows some text before and then after a section break was inserted after the line for Wednesday. The text for Thursday and Friday is on the next page but the dotted line indicates where that break was inserted. Section breaks won't print by the way.

Monday – 8am to 3pm

Tuesday – 8am to 1pm and 2pm to 3pm

Wednesday – 9am to 3pm

Thursday– 8am to 3pm

Friday – 10am to 12pm and 2pm to 3pm

Figure 2.15

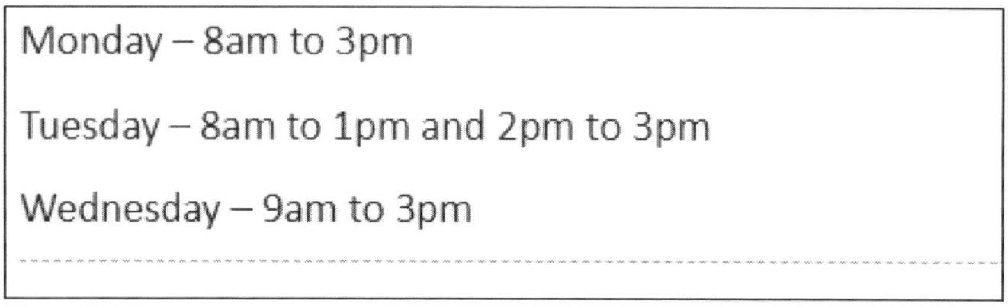

Monday – 8am to 3pm

Tuesday – 8am to 1pm and 2pm to 3pm

Wednesday – 9am to 3pm

Figure 2.16

Full screen – If you need more room on your screen and don't need to see things such as the toolbar or menu items then you can enable full screen mode. To get out of full screen mode simply press the *Esc* key on your keyboard.

Insert Menu

Docs will let you insert many types of items into your document, so you are not limited to only using text. Some of the more commonly inserted items include pictures and links to things such as websites etc.

Image – Use this option to insert pictures from various locations such as the internet, your computer, your Google Drive and so on.

Table – Tables are used to store information similar to how you would see it on a spreadsheet. Docs lets you insert tables up to 20x20 in size. I will be showing you how to use this feature in Chapter 3.

Drawing – If you are the artistic type and can actually draw using your computer then you can insert your own drawings into your document after you create them. You can also insert a drawing that you already have saved in your Google Drive folders. More on this in Chapter 3.

Chart – Docs will let you insert charts based on an existing Sheets spreadsheet file or you can insert a new chart into your document. You can insert a bar, column, line or pie chart. Once you insert a new chart it will automatically be linked to a new Sheets spreadsheet file that you can then edit with your own information by clicking on the link icon at the upper right corner of the chart.

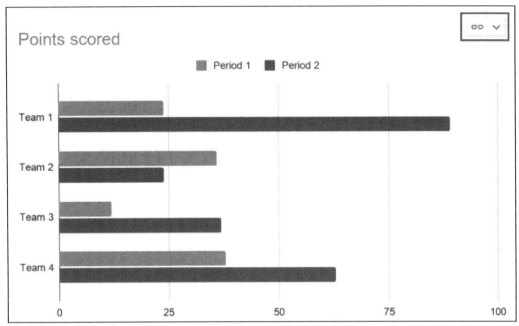

Figure 2.17

Horizontal Line – If you need to break up a section of your document then you can simply place your cursor where you want this break to be and insert a horizontal line.

Footnote – Footnotes are used to insert annotations at the bottom of a page to provide additional information about a specific part of your document. To insert a footnote you will need to place your cursor at the place in the document you want the footnote to refer to and then insert the footnote after that. As you can see in figure 2.18, there is a tiny 1 after the word process and then a matching 1 at the bottom of the page with the footnote text that refers to that part of the document.

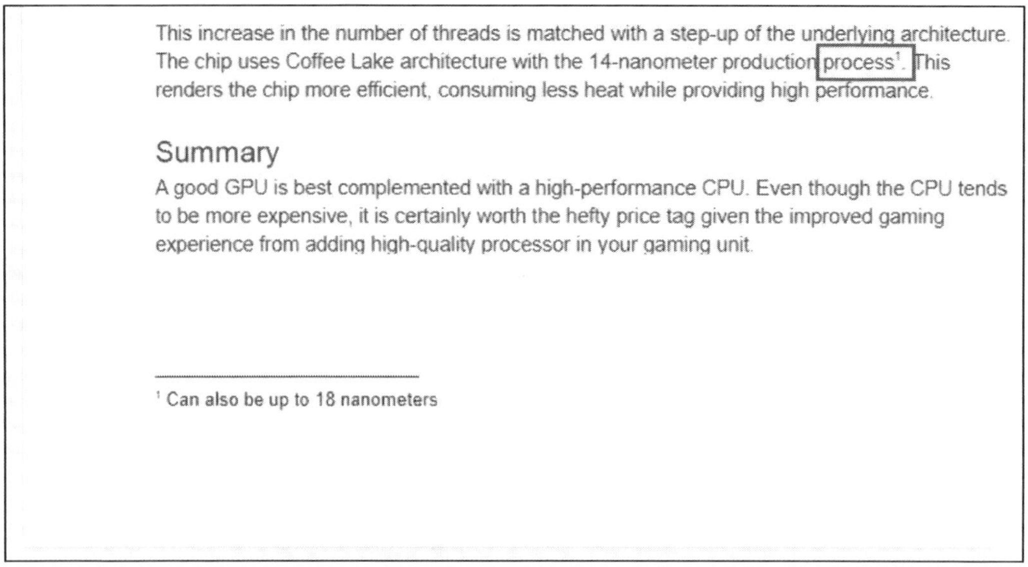

This increase in the number of threads is matched with a step-up of the underlying architecture. The chip uses Coffee Lake architecture with the 14-nanometer production process[1]. This renders the chip more efficient, consuming less heat while providing high performance.

Summary

A good GPU is best complemented with a high-performance CPU. Even though the CPU tends to be more expensive, it is certainly worth the hefty price tag given the improved gaming experience from adding high-quality processor in your gaming unit.

---

[1] Can also be up to 18 nanometers

Figure 2.18

Special Characters – Special characters are text based characters such as arrows, boxes, foreign language symbols and even emojis. You can search for a specific type of character and have it inserted into your document or even draw your own in the *Draw a symbol here* box and then have Docs search for a matching character.

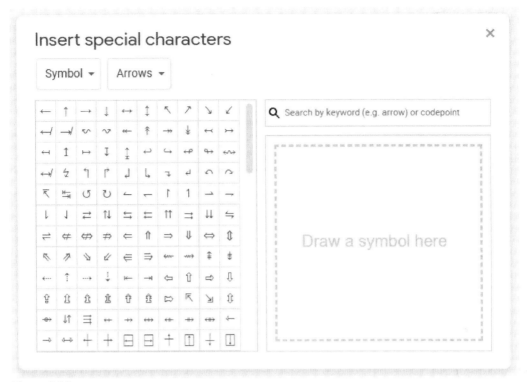

Figure 2.19

 If you are a Microsoft Windows user then you can do a search for **Character Map** and then have many additional types of special characters that you can then insert into your document. The characters from the Character Map are based off of what fonts you have installed on your computer.

Equation – This will let you type in mathematical equations into your document and will also enable the equation toolbar.

Headers & footers – Headers and footers are used for things such as chapter headings at the top of the page or document information at the bottom of the page. I will be going over how to use these in Chapter 4.

Page numbers – This is used to insert page numbers on each one of the pages within your document and Docs gives you several options on how you can insert these page numbers within your document. More on this in Chapter 4.

Break – You can insert several types of breaks into your document such as a page break or section break to help organize your information. I will be discussing the types of page breaks you can use in Chapter 3.

Link – Links can be used as a way to have a certain word or image take your reader to things such as websites or other documents by clicking on that word or image within your document. I will show you how to use links in Chapter 3.

Comment – When collaborating with other users on documents, you can insert comments to point out certain areas of your document or request others to make or approve your edits. I will be going over commenting in Chapter 5 when I discuss sharing and collaboration.

Bookmark – Bookmarks are similar to links but allow you to mark certain parts of your documents that you can then link to from other places in your documents. I will be going over bookmarks when I discuss links in Chapter 3.

Table of contents – If you are writing something such as a book that requires you to have a table of contents then you can have Docs create one for you based on your title and heading text. I will show you how to create a TOC in Chapter 4.

Format Menu

One of the most important things you should be doing with your documents is making sure that they are formatted correctly so they look professional and appealing to your readers. Formatting also ensures that your document is easy to read and doesn't appear like it was created by a 5 year old!

I will be going over most of these items in Chapter 4 so for now I will just give you a quick rundown of what each one of these items will do.

Text – This is another place you can go besides to toolbar to do things such as make your text bold or change its size. There are also additional options such as applying superscript or subscript to your text. Superscript looks like ^{this} while subscript looks like $_{this}$. If you need a quick way to change a bunch of text from lowercase to uppercase then you can highlight it all and choose the *Capitalization>UPPERCASE* option.

Paragraph styles – Here is where you can change your type to make it title text, heading text or normal text to help break your document into sections and to also help you create a table of contents or document outline.

Align & indent – These are the same options from the toolbar that I previously went over in this chapter.

Line spacing – I discussed line spacing a little when going over the toolbar items but what it does is allow you to change how much space is between lines or sentences within your document. There are several built in spacing settings and you can also add your own custom spacing amount if you desire. There are also options to change the spacing between paragraphs so if you would like extra spacing or less spacing between your paragraphs, you can adjust it from the menu item.

Columns – Docs has the ability to take existing text and convert it into 1, 2 or 3 columns if that is the style you are looking for.

Bullets & numbering – This is another way to make numbered or bulleted lists just like I showed you from the toolbar settings.

Headers & footers – Here is where you can apply custom formatting to your headers and footers if you do not like the default settings.

Page numbers – Here is where you can apply custom formatting to your page numbers if you do not like the default settings.

Table – If you have created a table, you can click on it and then go to this menu item to customize your table. You can do things such as insert or delete rows and columns, change border width and color and change cell background colors etc.

Image – Once you have an image inserted in your document, you can click on it and then use the options here to do things such as crop the image, rotate it, adjust the colors or replace the image with a different image etc.

Clear formatting – This will do the same thing as clicking on the Clear formatting button in the toolbar.

Borders & lines – If you have any borders around items such as images you can change things such as how thick the border is and if it uses a solid line or a dashed line.

Figure 2.20

Tools Menu

The Tools menu has some helpful options that will come in very handy as you are creating and working on your documents. You will most likely find yourself using these tools quite a bit.

Spelling & grammar – We all make mistakes when we type so it's always a good idea to let the software check out spelling and grammar. Just keep in mind that you don't have to approve any "fixes" that Docs suggests if you don't agree with them. I will show you how to use this tool in Chapter 4.

Word count – If you need to know how many words or even how many characters are in your document you can use this option to show you that information. If you check the box that says Display word count while typing then you will get a

38

little box at the lower left of the screen that will update your word count as you are typing.

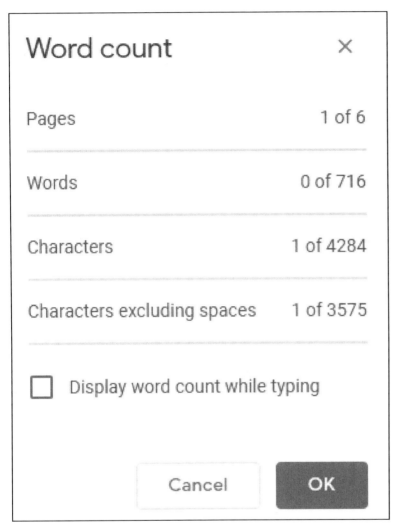

Figure 2.21

Review suggested edits – When you are working in Suggestion mode you can suggest changes to the document and then someone else can approve or reject your suggestions. Using this option will show all of the suggested edits for your document. Figure 2.22 shows an example of a suggested edit. I will be going over the three Docs modes in Chapter 5.

Figure 2.22

Compare documents – If you have two of the same document but there were changes made to one or both of them then you can have Docs do a comparison between the documents to show you the differences. I will demonstrate this process in Chapter 7.

Citations – If you use the Explorer feature (discussed in Chapter 3), you can use information you find online within your document and you have the option to use citations to give credit to the owners of the content. This option will let you see your current citations.

Explore – The Explore tool allows you to search files in your Drive as well as find content online without having to leave your document. I will show you how this works in Chapter 3.

Linked objects – If you have linked any external content to your document such as a chart from a spreadsheet or a drawing from your Google Drive then you can view a listing of your linked objects by using this option.

Dictionary – If you would like to know the definition of a word or see any synonyms for that word you can highlight it and then use the Dictionary option to see this information.

Figure 2.23

Voice typing – If you have a microphone attached to your computer or are using your mobile device with its built in microphone then you can speak into your mic and have your voice translated to text on the page. I will be going over this in more detail in Chapter 3.

Script editor – This option is for developers and programmers who want to add additional features to Docs by writing code for the app.

Preferences – Here you can check or uncheck some options for how Docs works for you such as having it automatically correct your spelling etc. All of the options are checked by default in the *General* section.

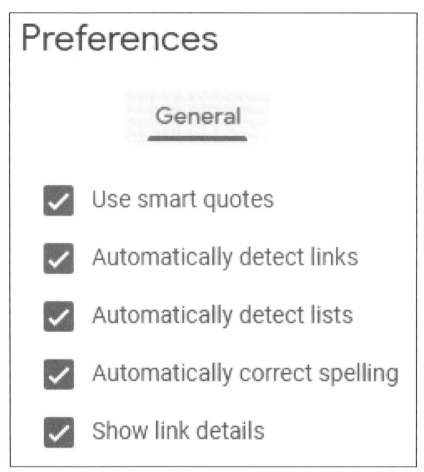

Figure 2.24

The *Substitutions* section has some built in text substitutions like automatically replacing (c) with © or 1/2 with ½ . In Chapter 7 I will show you how to create your own custom substitutions to cut down on the amount of typing you need to do.

Accessibility settings – If you need assistance using Docs then you can check out the accessibility settings to do things such as turn on braille support or the screen magnifier.

Accessibility settings

☐ **Turn on screen reader support**

Required for braille support and collaborator announcements ⑦

    ☐ Turn on braille support

    Works with third-party braille hardware

    ☐ Turn on collaborator announcements

    Know when people enter and exit your files

☐ **Turn on screen magnifier support**

Works with third-party screen magnifier software ⑦

Figure 2.25

There isn't much to the Help menu besides searching for help topics but there is one choice that I wanted to mention. If you go to the Help menu, you will see an option for *Training*. Clicking on this will take you to the Docs training website where you can check out some additional training resources.

Chapter 3 - Creating Documents

Now that we are done with the tedious process of going over the toolbar and menu items, it's time to have a little fun and start creating some of our own documents! In this chapter I will be going over how to create a document from scratch and add items such as pictures, drawings and tables etc. as well as how to do things such as create links and finally print out your document.

I will also be going over how to use the built in templates available with Docs and will also show you how to open other types of documents that were not created with Docs.

Using Templates

Before I get into creating a document from scratch, I wanted to go over how to use the built in Docs templates because they can save you a lot of time since much of the work has already been done for you because they already have the basic layout and formatting in place based on the type of template you choose to start with.

To open a template file, simply go to the *File* menu and then choose *New>From template*. Then you will be shown any templates you have recently used as well as additional templates organized into categories as seen in figure 3.1.

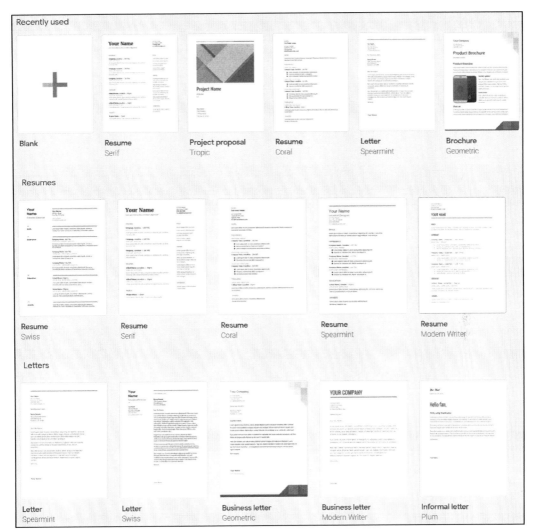

Figure 3.1

To use a template, all you need to do is click on the one you want to use, and it will open within Docs. So if I choose the *Resume-Swiss* template (figure 3.2) it will open, and I will then be able to start editing it to make it my own. Notice how Docs has placeholder words that don't make much sense in the template. This is only used to show you the format and layout of the template and you would replace this text with your own.

Your Name

Creative Director

— Skills

— Experience

— Education

— Awards

Your Name
123 Your Street
Your City, ST 12345

123.456.7890
no_reply@example.com

Lorem ipsum dolor sit amet, consectetur adipiscing elit. Aenean ac interdum nisi. Sed in consequat mi. Sed pulvinar lacinia felis eu finibus.

Company Name / Job Title
MONTH 20XX - PRESENT, LOCATION

Lorem ipsum dolor sit amet, consectetur adipiscing elit. Aenean ac interdum nisi. Sed in consequat mi. Sed in consequat mi, sed pulvinar lacinia felis eu finibus.

Company Name / Job Title
MONTH 20XX - MONTH 20XX, LOCATION

Lorem ipsum dolor sit amet, consectetur adipiscing elit. Aenean ac interdum nisi. Sed in consequat mi.

Company Name / Job Title
MONTH 20XX - MONTH 20XX, LOCATION

Lorem ipsum dolor sit amet, consectetur adipiscing elit. Aenean ac interdum nisi. Sed in consequat mi. Sed pulvinar lacinia felis eu finibus.

School Name / Degree
MONTH 20XX - MONTH 20XX, LOCATION

Lorem ipsum dolor sit amet, consectetuer adipiscing elit, sed diam nonummy nibh euismod tincidunt ut laoreet dolore.

School Name / Degree
MONTH 20XX - MONTH 20XX, LOCATION

Lorem ipsum dolor sit amet, consectetuer adipiscing elit, sed diam nonummy nibh euismod tincidunt ut laoreet dolore.

Lorem ipsum dolor sit amet, consectetur adipiscing elit. Aenean ac interdum nisi. Sed in consequat mi. Sed pulvinar lacinia felis eu finibus.

Figure 3.2

 When working with templates, it's a good idea to rename the template to something that will make more sense to you. This will also place the document in your Drive folder where you can access it later to continue to work it.

You can also create your own template files if you have a particular form etc. that you like to use over and over. Simply create a new file and format the document the way you like it. Then give it a name that includes template and save it to your Google Drive. You can also create a new folder in your Drive just for templates and then move your new custom template document into that folder. I will be discussing using Google Drive in more detail in Chapter 6.

Opening Other Document Types
One other thing I wanted to quickly discuss before starting a new document from scratch was how to open existing documents that were not made using Google Docs.

When you go to *File* and *Open* you will be taken directly to your Google Drive and be shown the files and folders within your Drive as shown in figure 3.3. By default you will only be shown documents, and this is because there is a Documents filter applied as you can see in the search box with the word *Documents* with an X next to it.

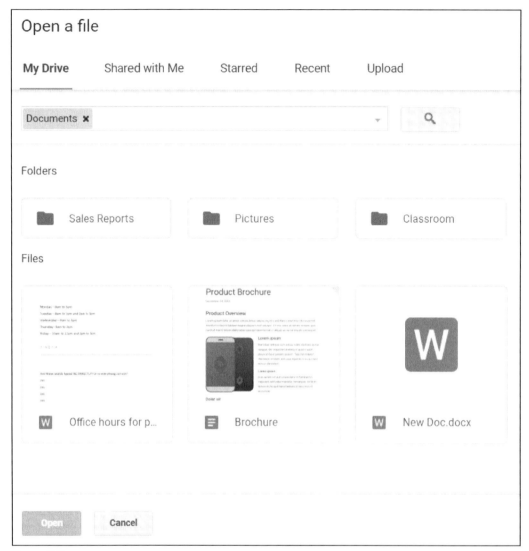

Figure 3.3

If you click on the X next to Documents to remove the filter then you will be shown all of your files as seen in figure 3.4. You might have other file types such as spreadsheets, PDF files, presentation files and so on within your Drive.

Now just because you can store any type of file in your Google Drive doesn't mean that Docs will be able to open it, but it does do a good job at opening many other types of files such as Word documents and PDF files and if it can't open the file in Docs then it will try and open it in the correct app for you so you can still access it. For example, if you click on a Sheets file (Google spreadsheet app), it will automatically open the file using Google Sheets.

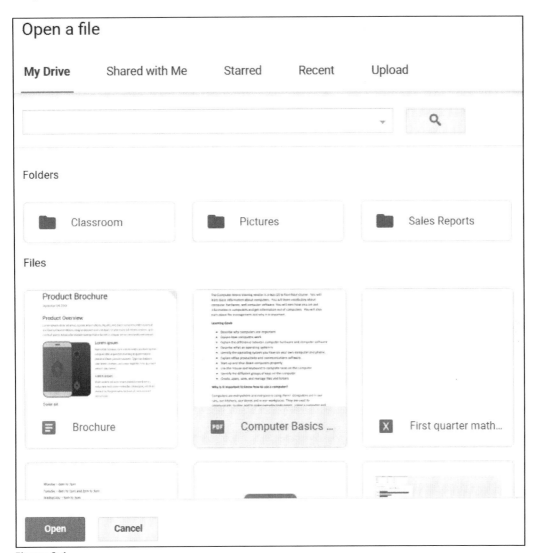

Figure 3.4

If you need to open a file on your computer that is not stored online in your Google Drive then you would click on *Upload* and then browse to the location on your computer where you have the file stored and open it that way. Or you can simply drag it into the upload box as seen in figure 3.5.

Figure 3.5

 Once you upload a file into Docs, it will then be stored in your Google Drive for easy access later on so be aware that you will have a copy on your local hard drive as well as in Drive so always make sure you are working on the correct copy.

Starting Your First Document

Now that you know how to open a template file or a preexisting file from your Google Drive or your computer I would like to take a minute to go over how to start a new document from scratch.

To start a new blank document, simply go to the File menu and choose *New>Document.* You might notice that you can also create other types of files from here such as a Sheets spreadsheet or a Slides presentation file. If you do choose one of these other file types, Docs will open the appropriate app so you can start working right away rather than having to open the corresponding app first.

Once you have your new document open, it will be a blank page that is ready for you to start typing on and it will be set to use the default font, font size, line spacing, margins, paper size and so on. If you change attributes such as the font or font size, it will keep those attributes for as long as you keep typing. But once you change the font or size etc., it will keep the new setting until you change it to something else again.

I always like to configure my document right away so I know how things will be looking as I am working on it because if you start changing things like margins and font size later on you might find that you will need to go through the entire document to make sure things are looking right.

The default name of your new document will be *Untitled document* so you might want to change it right away so if you end up closing the document it will be easy to find when you need to go back to it since it will have a more descriptive name. To rename your document, simply click in the document name box and type in a new name. Docs will automatically update your document name within your Google Drive.

Figure 3.6

If you have already added some text before you rename your document, you might find that Docs will use that text as the document name trying to help you out. So if that's the case, just delete what it puts in there and add your own unless you like the suggestion it came up with.

As you are typing in the name of the document you will see that after the name it says *in My Drive* as seen in figure 3.7. Then after you type in the name and click off the name box it changes to a folder as seen in figure 3.8. Clicking on either one of these will allow you to change where you want to save your new document as seen in figure 3.8. If you have any folders in your Drive you can save it to one of those folders or you can click the *new folder* icon at the bottom to create a new folder to save your document to.

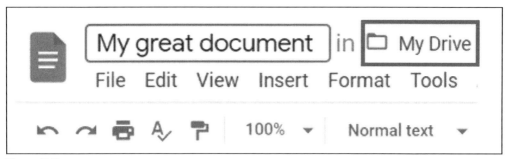

Figure 3.7

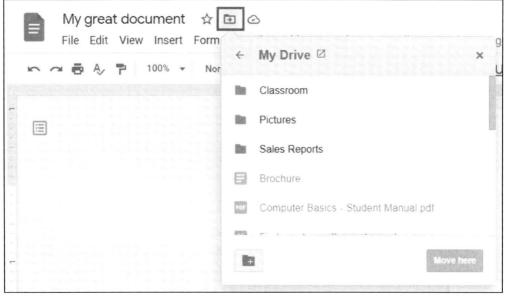

Figure 3.8

As you are working on your document you will notice at the top of the page that it tells you the last time you made a change. This timestamp will also be shown in your Google Drive telling you the last time it was saved since Docs saves your work every time you make an edit.

Figure 3.9

One other thing you should be aware of when working on your document is that you should be in *Editing* mode when making changes. This is shown underneath the *Share* button at the top right of the page and is the default mode. There are also suggesting and viewing modes and I will be going over all of the modes in Chapter 5.

Figure 3.10

Voice Typing

If you are the type who doesn't like to type or is not the fastest typist in the world then you are in luck. Docs has an option that allows you to use the microphone attached to your computer (if you have one) or the built in microphone on your smartphone or tablet to translate what you say into text within your document.

To use Voice typing simply go to the *Tools* menu and then select *Voice typing* and the Voice typing microphone will appear and all you need to do is click on the microphone icon and start speaking and Docs will add the text as you speak.

Figure 3.11

The first time you try and use Voice typing, you might get a popup in your web browser asking for permission for Docs to use your microphone and you will need to click on the *Allow* button otherwise you won't be able to use this feature.

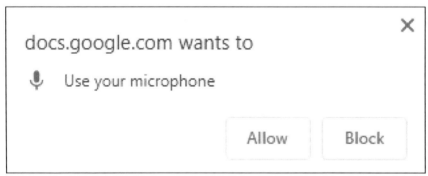

Figure 3.12

Once you grant access to Docs to use your microphone, you will notice that the microphone icon turns red and then you just need to start talking and the text will be added to your document. When you are finished, simply click the microphone icon again to stop.

Figure 3.13

The translation most likely won't be perfect so it's a good idea to proofread what was typed out to make sure that it matches what you said. You can even say things like "period" to add a (.) to the end of a sentence or "new line' to have the cursor go down to the next line.

Inserting Images\Pictures
There is a very good chance that you will be inserting some type of picture into your document and fortunately Docs makes this easy to do and allows you to insert your image from a variety of sources. When you go to the *Insert* menu and then to *Image*, you will have several options to choose from.

Upload from computer – This option lets you browse your local hard drive to upload a file that you have stored on your computer. You will need to know where you have this file to use this method of course.

Search the web – If you don't have a picture of the object you want to use on your local computer then you can search the internet and find it that way. Docs will use Google Images for your search so all you need to do is type in what you are looking for and when you find it, simply click on the picture or pictures you want to insert into your document and click on INSERT at the bottom of the search results (figure 3.14). You can also drag and drop any of the pictures right into your document.

Figure 3.14

Drive – If you have the picture you want to use stored in your Google Drive then you can insert it from there into your document. When you use the Drive option you will be shown your recent files, and also have an option to see all of the files within your Drive (My Drive). You will also see an option named *shared with me* that will show you files that others have shared with you in case you want to use one of those.

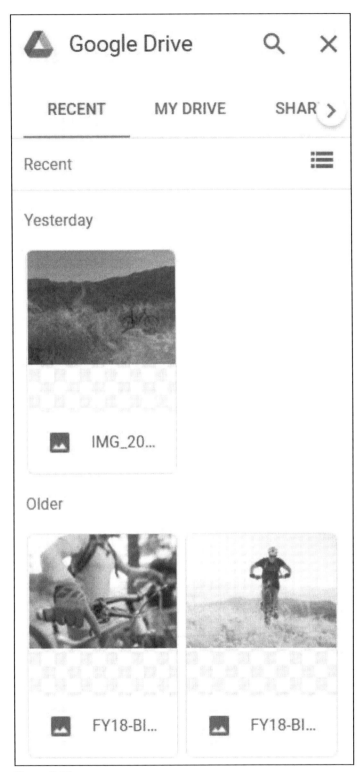

Figure 3.15

Photos – The Photos option refers to Google Photos which is an online storage repository that you can use with your Google account that allows you to store and organize your pictures into albums. If you have an Android based smartphone then there is a good chance you are already using Google Photos and might not even know it. Some models will automatically upload your pictures to your Google Photos account so if this is not what you want then you might want to log into your Photos account and remove any pictures you don't want to be stored "in the cloud".

Figure 3.16

 If you have an Android smartphone and would like to improve your phone skills then check out my book titled **Android Smartphones Made Easy.**
https://www.amazon.com/dp/1086026837

URL – If you know of a picture that you have seen on a particular website then you can also use the address of that picture to have it inserted into your document. A URL (Uniform Resource Locator) is another name for a website address such as www.onlinecomputertips.com and when you see images on websites, they will each have their own unique URL and how you get this URL will vary a little depending on what web browser you are using.

What I like to do to get an image URL or address is right click on the image and choose *Copy image address* and then paste it wherever I need to use it. I use the Google Chrome web browser so the wording might be a little different in another web browser.

Once you have the image address, you can then use the URL option for inserting an image and then paste in the address and click the INSERT button.

Figure 3.17

Camera – Finally we have the Camera option which will let you insert a picture right from your camera if you have one attached to your computer. If you are using Docs on your smartphone or tablet then you can use its camera to take and insert an image right on the spot.

Inserting Tables

Tables are a great way to store information in an organized fashion. They can be used in the same way many people use spreadsheets to enter data or create lists. Docs will let you easily create a table up to a size of 20 by 20 cells. When I say cell, that is the box that you enter your information into.

To create a table, go to the *Insert* menu and then choose *Table* and drag your mouse over the boxes until you get to the size table you wish to insert. Figure 3.18 shows that a table size of 4x3 will be created and figure 3.19 shows the results. The cell size will be determined by how large you make your tables and by your page size.

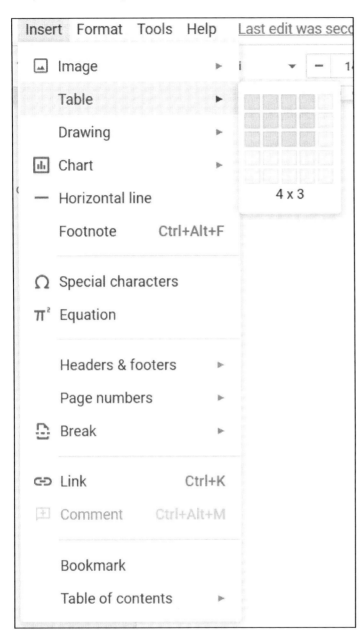

Figure 3.18

Figure 3.19

Each cell will have an arrow symbol that you can click on to add borders around one or multiple cells. The cursor in the top cell indicates which cell you will be typing in and can be moved to any cell with a click of the mouse.

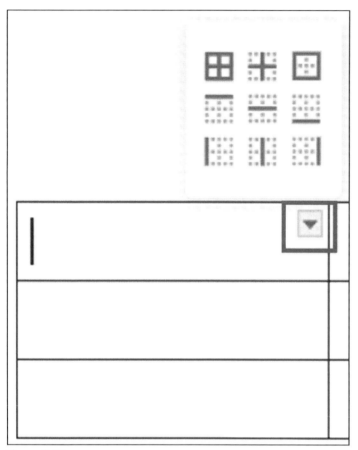

Figure 3.20

Next I will enter some data into my cells to create my table. Once you enter your text you can format it just like you would any other text. You can make it bold, change the type size, change the font and so on.

Product 1 Sales	Product 2 Sales	Product 3 Sales	Product 4 Sales
25	32	27	37
18	43	36	41

Figure 3.21

If you need to resize a row or column then all you need to do is position your mouse so it makes a double arrow icon as seen in figure 3.22. Then you can increase or decrease the row or column size by dragging your mouse in the appropriate direction.

Product 1 Sales	Product 2 Sales
25 ←‖→	32
18	43

Figure 3.22

If you need to add or delete rows or columns then make sure your mouse is in the appropriate part of your table and then right click on the table itself. You will then see options to insert rows and columns as well as delete them (figure 3.23).

Insert row above

Insert row below

Insert column left

Insert column right

Delete row

Delete column

Delete table

Distribute rows

Distribute columns

Table properties

Figure 3.23

If you click on *Table properties* you will get some additional formatting options such as the ability to change the table border, add background colors to your cells, change cell alignment and so on.

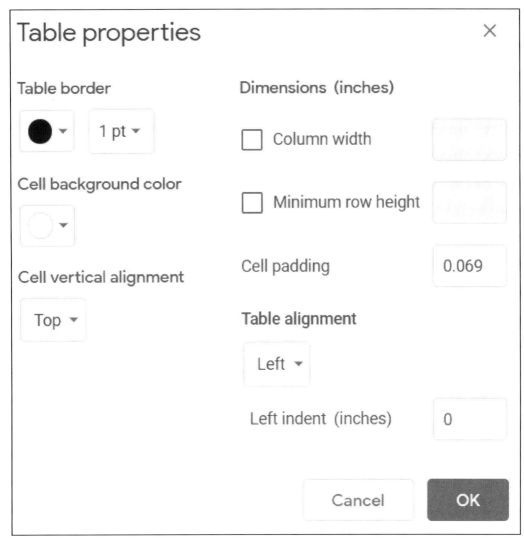

Figure 3.24

Figure 3.25 shows my table after adding a colored background to the top row and a thicker overall border to the entire table.

Product 1 Sales	Product 2 Sales	Product 3 Sales	Product 4 Sales
25	32	27	37
18	43	36	41

Figure 3.25

Inserting Drawings

If you are the artistic type or happen to have a Google Drawing that you previously created or that someone created for you then you can insert your drawing into your document. I don't find this too useful but if you need to make a point with an illustration then you might want to check out this feature.

When you go to the *Insert* menu and choose *Drawing* and then *New* you will be presented with a blank "canvas" that you can then create your drawing on. Once you are in your new drawing you can add things such as lines, shapes, images, text and so on to create your drawing. Once you have it looking the way you like then simply click on *Save and Close* to have the drawing inserted into your document.

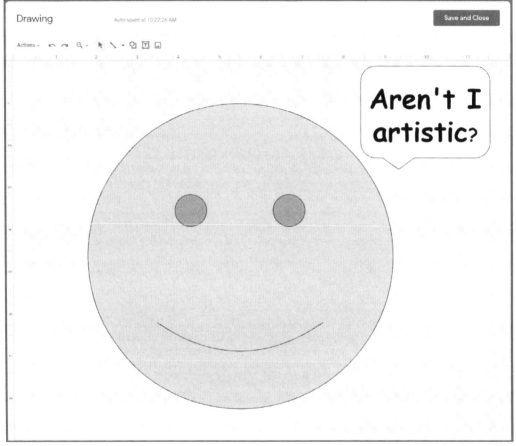

Figure 3.26

Once you have your drawing inserted into your document you can edit it by clicking on it to highlight it and then clicking on the *Edit* button as seen in figure

3.27. This will then open your drawing in the drawing app where you can make your changes and then you will need to click on *Save* and *Close* again to have your changes updated within your document.

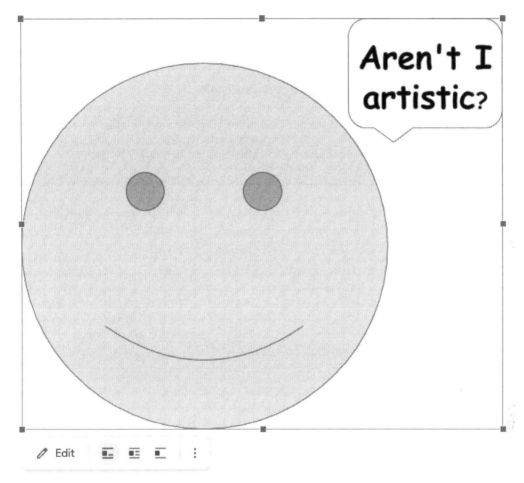

Figure 3.27

Next to the Edit button, you will find the text wrapping options where you can configure your text to do things such as wrap around the drawing or be in line with the text etc. If you click the three vertical dots you will have options for things like rotating or resizing your drawing on the page.

If you have any drawings stored in your Google Drive you can insert those as well from the *Insert>Drawing>From Drive* option. When you insert a drawing from your Drive then you will have the option to keep the drawing in Docs linked to your original drawing or insert it as unlinked. If you choose the *Link to source* option then any changes you make to your drawing in Docs will be updated to your drawing stored in your Drive.

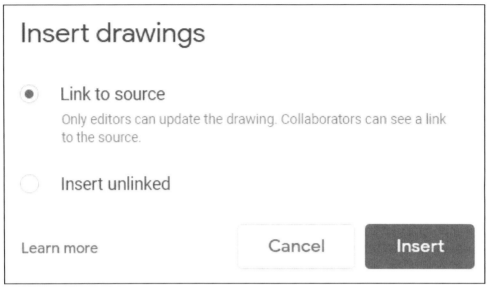

Figure 3.28

Inserting Breaks

As you work on your document you might find that you would like certain text to be on different pages or different sections and this is where you will use page breaks and section breaks to accomplish this.

Page breaks simply add a new blank page to your document so if you want to continue your work on a new page you would go to the **Insert** menu and then choose *Breaks>Page break*. Just make sure that your mouse cursor is located where you want the new page to be inserted otherwise you will end up splitting your text up on to two different pages.

Section breaks work differently than page breaks and are used to split your document into different "sections" where you can then have different margins, headers and footers for that particular section. For example, if you are writing a book and want to have named chapter headers for every page in that particular chapter you would use section breaks, otherwise you would have the same header for every page\chapter in your book.

There are two types of section breaks you can use in Docs and they are *next page* and *continuous*. Next page will insert a section break and split your text onto the next page where you insert the break while a continuous break will insert a break yet leave your text on the same page.

Inserting Links

Anyone who has used a web browser to access the internet has clicked on a link to take you to another page on a particular website or to take you to a different website altogether. Docs will let you insert links into your document that will allow you to do the same type of thing. You can add links that will take your reader to a particular website, a different location within your document or another document altogether.

To create a link to a website, simply place your cursor where you would like the link to be created and then go to the *Insert* menu and choose *Link*. Next, you will need to type in the text you want to be displayed for your link and then also the website address itself. As you start typing, Docs will start searching online to find a match for the website you are adding.

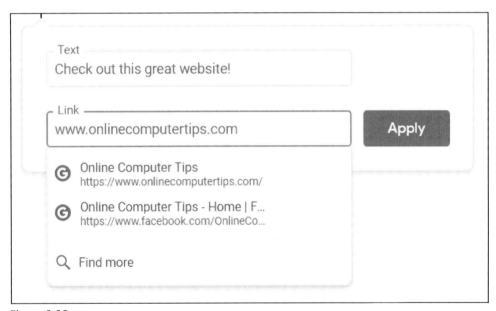

Figure 3.29

Once you have things the way you like, click the *Apply* button and your new website link will be inserted into your document. Then the reader can click on that text to be taken directly to that website. The link text will be blue and also underlined as seen at the bottom of figure 3.30.

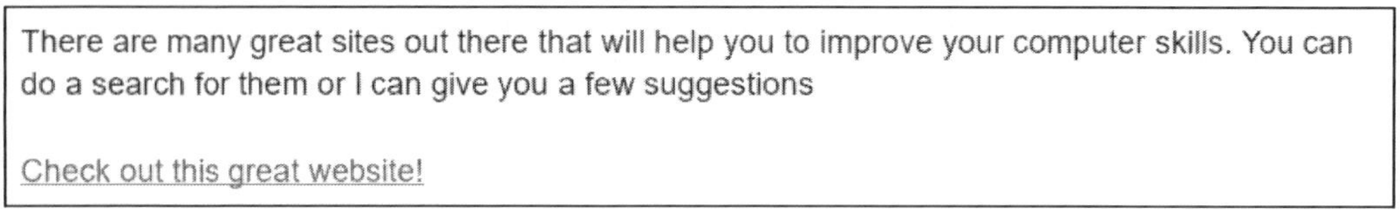

There are many great sites out there that will help you to improve your computer skills. You can do a search for them or I can give you a few suggestions

Check out this great website!

Figure 3.30

You don't have to have custom text for your website link if you don't want to. You can have the link text be the same as the address itself by typing in the website address in the text box as well. Or you can copy the address from the Link box and paste it into the text box to speed up the process.

You can also choose existing word or words to create a link with. Simply highlight the text you want to use for your link and then follow the same process.

There are many great sites out there that will help you to improve your computer skills. You can do a search for them or I can give you a few suggestions.

Text
suggestions

Link
https://www.onlinecomputertips.com/   Apply

Figure 3.31

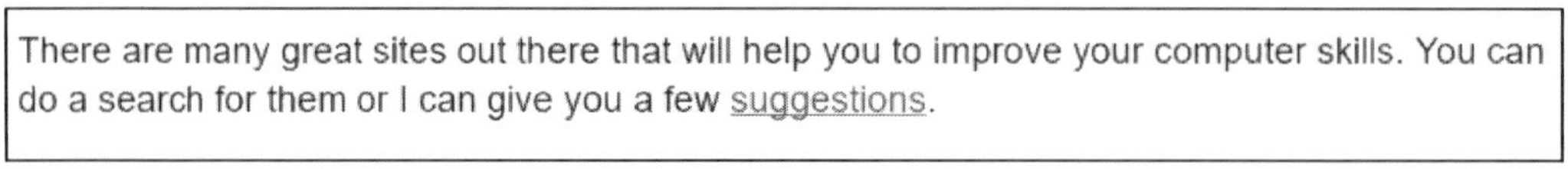

There are many great sites out there that will help you to improve your computer skills. You can do a search for them or I can give you a few suggestions.

Figure 3.32

You can also do the same thing with images by selecting them and then turning them into a clickable link as seen in figure 3.33.

Figure 3.33

Docs allows you to create bookmarks within your document that you can then go back to and create a link for. So that way your reader can click on a link that will take them to the corresponding part of the document.

To create a bookmark you will need to highlight the text (or image) that you want to use for a bookmark and from the *Insert* menu choose *Bookmark*. Docs will then insert a blue bookmark icon next to that text or image as you can see in the bottom of figure 3.34 where it says *CPU Shopping Tips*.

Then when you want to create a link to that bookmark, you will follow the same process as before, but you will now have a *Bookmarks* option where you can choose from the bookmarks that you have created within your document.

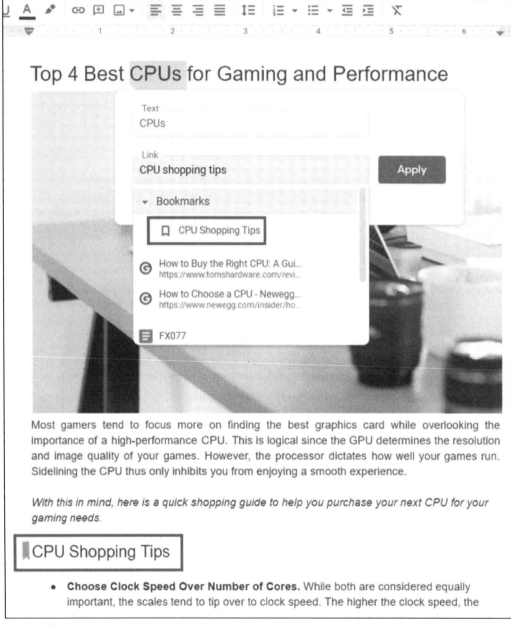

You can also create bookmarks that point to other documents that you have stored in your Google Drive folder. If you start to type in some text that is related to one of your other documents then Docs will try and find any matching documents that you might have in your drive. Figure 3.35 shows what happens when I type in vpn in the link box and how Docs will find not only websites that match that text but also documents from my Drive that might be a match.

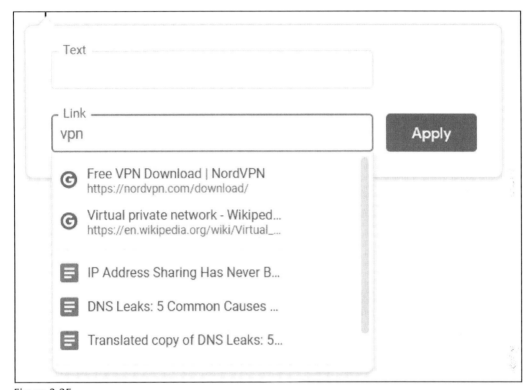

Figure 3.35

Then when I click on my new link I will be able to open the linked document right from my existing document. I can also open a preview of the document as well as copy, edit or remove the link.

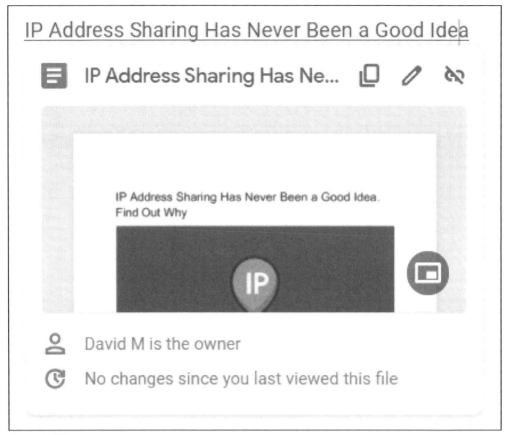

Figure 3.36

I will be going over how to create links from within your Google Drive in Chapter 5 when I discuss document collaboration.

Creating Columns

If you are designing something like a brochure or other type of publication that would benefit from having the information in a column format then you can do that fairly easily within Docs.

If you already have the text in your document then it's easy to put the text into columns. All you need to do is highlight the text you want to convert to a column format and then go to the *Format* menu and choose *Columns* and then tell Docs how many columns to put the text into.

1. Web Applications

Why install and use the office when you can get everything you want with applications like Google Docs, Adobe's Buzzword or Zoho or Peepel. Any kind of work can be taken from today's web applications that work within the browser.

2. Defragmentation

It accelerates the ability of a computer to work by combining scattered data into your computer. The way files are stored on a computer also slows down modern hard disks. As files are saved or deleted on the hard disk, all this data is stored on different parts of the hard disk instead of being stored together. As a result, access to files is slowed down. Configuring these blocks of information scattered on disk not only increases the available space in memory but also makes it easier to access information.

3. Set Passwords

Regarding the choice of passwords that will be used to protect the PC, I suggest using passwords that are long enough, difficult to guess (therefore completely meaningless) and contain numbers, letters, and symbols. You can find out more about the strong titles you have developed for this topic.

Figure 3.37

The default settings are 1, 2 or 3 columns and for my example I will choose the 3 column setting.

Figure 3.38

Figure 3.39 shows my text after it has been changed to a column format. Docs will spread out the text to make it fit the number of columns the best it can.

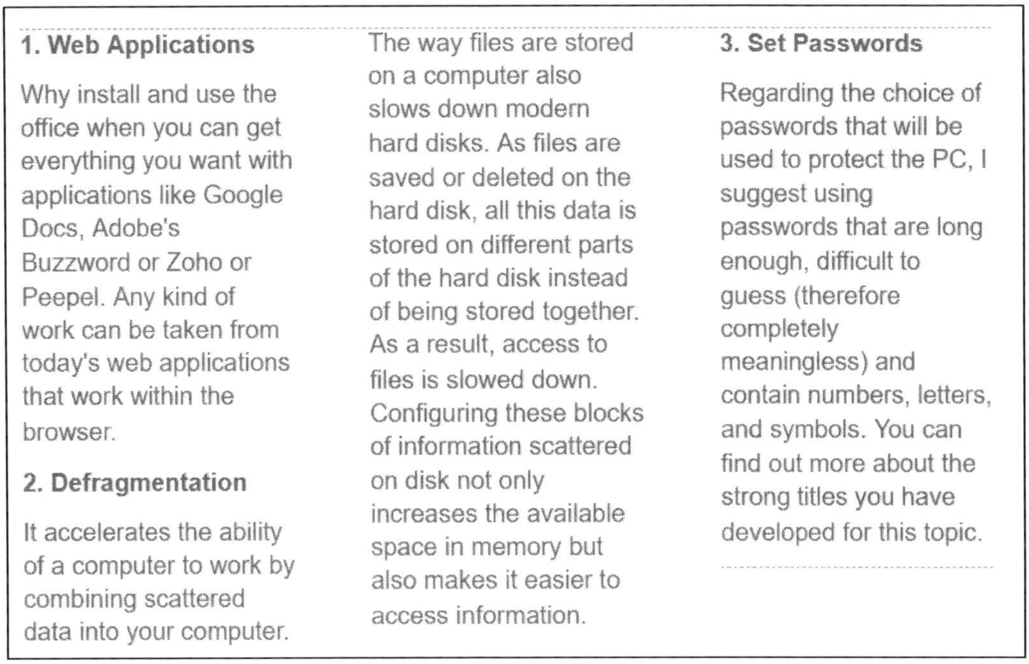

1. Web Applications

Why install and use the office when you can get everything you want with applications like Google Docs, Adobe's Buzzword or Zoho or Peepel. Any kind of work can be taken from today's web applications that work within the browser.

2. Defragmentation

It accelerates the ability of a computer to work by combining scattered data into your computer. The way files are stored on a computer also slows down modern hard disks. As files are saved or deleted on the hard disk, all this data is stored on different parts of the hard disk instead of being stored together. As a result, access to files is slowed down. Configuring these blocks of information scattered on disk not only increases the available space in memory but also makes it easier to access information.

3. Set Passwords

Regarding the choice of passwords that will be used to protect the PC, I suggest using passwords that are long enough, difficult to guess (therefore completely meaningless) and contain numbers, letters, and symbols. You can find out more about the strong titles you have developed for this topic.

Figure 3.39

When you click on the *Format>Columns* and then click on *More options* (figure 3.40) you can choose the number of columns you want to use (up to 3) as well as the spacing between the columns. I like to check the box that says *Line between columns* so Docs will put a fine line in between each of the columns to make the columns stand out a little more (figure 3.41).

Figure 3.40

1. Web Applications

Why install and use the office when you can get everything you want with applications like Google Docs, Adobe's Buzzword or Zoho or Peepel. Any kind of work can be taken from today's web applications that work within the browser.

2. Defragmentation

It accelerates the ability of a computer to work by combining scattered data into your computer.

The way files are stored on a computer also slows down modern hard disks. As files are saved or deleted on the hard disk, all this data is stored on different parts of the hard disk instead of being stored together. As a result, access to files is slowed down. Configuring these blocks of information scattered on disk not only increases the available space in memory but also makes it easier to access information.

3. Set Passwords

Regarding the choice of passwords that will be used to protect the PC, I suggest using passwords that are long enough, difficult to guess (therefore completely meaningless) and contain numbers, letters, and symbols. You can find out more about the strong titles you have developed for this topic.

Figure 3.41

If you need to adjust the text in your columns so that it's organized a little better then you can do so by putting line spaces in between your text. Just be aware that your column sizes might not be the same as seen in figure 3.42.

1. Web Applications	2. Defragmentation	3. Set Passwords
Why install and use the office when you can get everything you want with applications like Google Docs, Adobe's Buzzword or Zoho or Peepel. Any kind of work can be taken from today's web applications that work within the browser.	It accelerates the ability of a computer to work by combining scattered data into your computer. The way files are stored on a computer also slows down modern hard disks. As files are saved or deleted on the hard disk, all this data is stored on different parts of the hard disk instead of being stored together. As a result, access to files is slowed down. Configuring these blocks of information scattered on disk not only increases the available space in memory but also makes it easier to access information.	Regarding the choice of passwords that will be used to protect the PC, I suggest using passwords that are long enough, difficult to guess (therefore completely meaningless) and contain numbers, letters, and symbols. You can find out more about the strong titles you have developed for this topic.

Figure 3.42

Explore Button

You might have noticed the Explore button at the lower right hand corner of the screen while working on your document. You might have also seen it while in the Tools menu and wondered what it was used for.

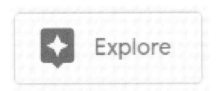

When you type in a search term in the Explore box you will have three sources to find information related to that search term. Docs will search the web, Google

Images and also your Drive to see if it can find anything that might match. So if I type in *Computer tips* I get a variety of results in all three locations.

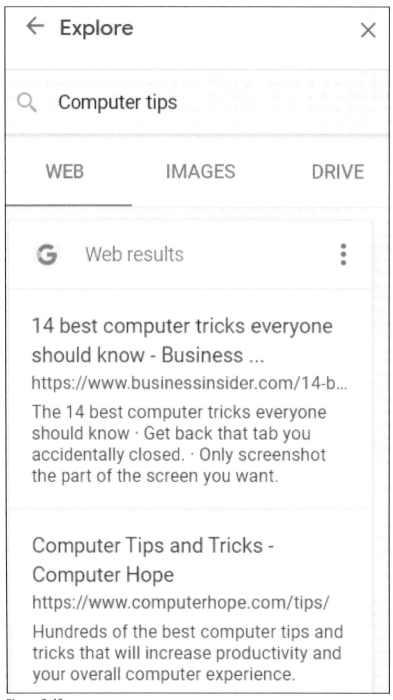

Figure 3.43

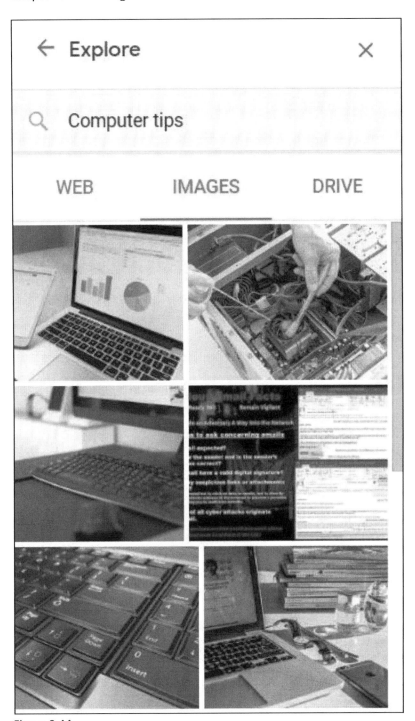

Figure 3.44

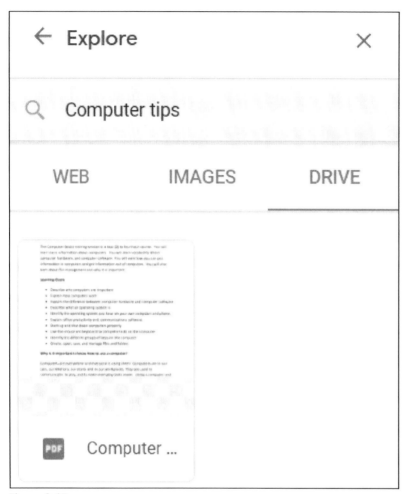

Figure 3.45

If I click on one of the Web results then I can use information from that page in my document as long as I give credit (cite) to the owner of that information. To cite my reference all I need to do is click on the cite (double quote) symbol that I will get when hovering over one of the results as shown in figure 3.46. Then Docs will put a footnote at the bottom of that page with a reference number at the end of the text in the document and at the beginning of the footnote (figure 3.47).

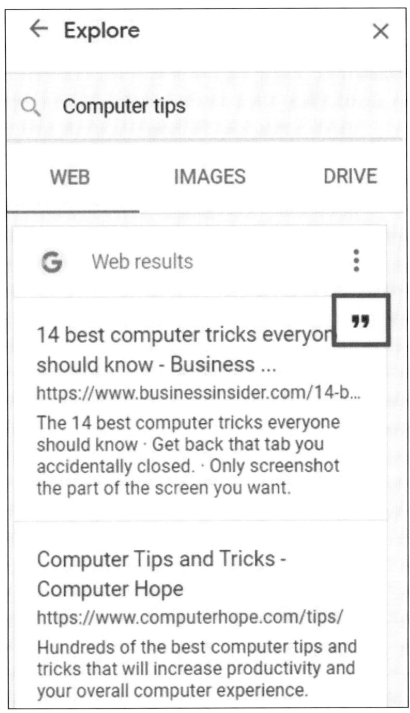

Figure 3.46

If you want to get back a tab you closed, just press "Control" (or "Command" on Mac), plus "Shift," plus "T," and it will magically reappear[1]

---

[1] 14 best computer tricks everyone should know - Business ...." 26 Nov. 2015, https://www.businessinsider.com/14-best-computer-tricks-everyone-should-know. Accessed 23 Dec. 2020.

Figure 3.47

If I would like to use an image that I found from my search results then all I need to do is simply drag and drop the image into my document or hover over the image and use the *Insert image* option.

It's always a good idea to cite any images you use as well just to make sure you are covered legally unless of course it's for a document that will never be published or really seen by anyone who might want to make a fuss about it. There is no cite option for images so you would have to create the citation manually.

If you would like to use some information found in a document on your Drive then you can click on that document to open it up and then copy and paste the information you need into your document.

Printing Your Documents

Once you have your document looking pristine, there is a good chance you are going to want to print it out on paper. Yes many people just email and share their documents but some of us still like to print them out too!

Printing your document is very easy to do but there are some things you might want to check during the printing process to make sure your print job comes out the way you want it to.

When you go to the *File* menu and then click on *Print* you will be shown a print preview of your document as well as some basic settings that you can change.

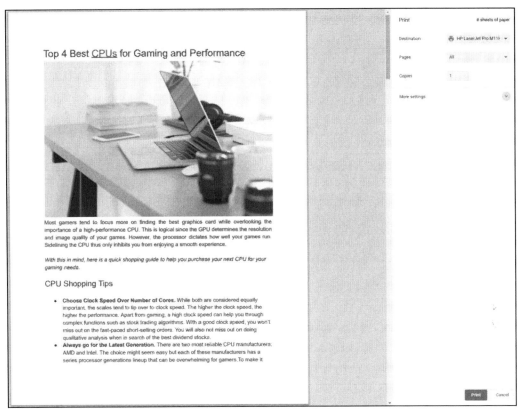

Figure 3.48

You can scroll down the pages to see how they will look when printed and at the top right of the print dialog box you will see how many pages will be printed. In my case it says 6 sheets of paper meaning my document is 6 pages long.

The *Destination* section will let you choose which of your printers you will print to assuming you have more than one. You will also have the option to print to a PDF file or save the document to your Google Drive.

The *Pages* area will let you determine which pages will be printed and is set to all by default. If you change it to Custom you can tell Docs exactly which pages you want to print. For example you can enter **2-5** to print pages 2 through 5 or you can enter **1-3, 6** to print pages 1 through 3 and also print page 6.

The *copies* selection will let you determine how many copies of your document to print.

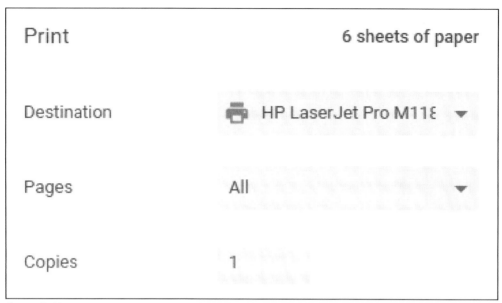

Figure 3.49

To get some additional printing choices you can click on *More settings* and then fine tune your print job from there. Here you can adjust some of the page formatting such as the paper size and margins if you are trying to fit your print job on a different size sheet of paper than what you created it with in Docs.

The *Scale* choice comes in handy because it will help you fit your page onto a specific size sheet of paper if things are not fitting the way you want them to. When using this option you can type in a percentage of the size to try and make it fit. For example you can have your document printed at 75% of its original size or 130% of its original size. As you adjust this number, the print preview will change to reflect the new size.

If your printer supports two sided printing then you can check the box that says *Print on both sides* and Docs will use both sides of each sheet of paper for your print job to save paper.

The *Background graphics* checkbox is enabled by default so if you have any background watermarks or images that you don't want to print, you can uncheck this box.

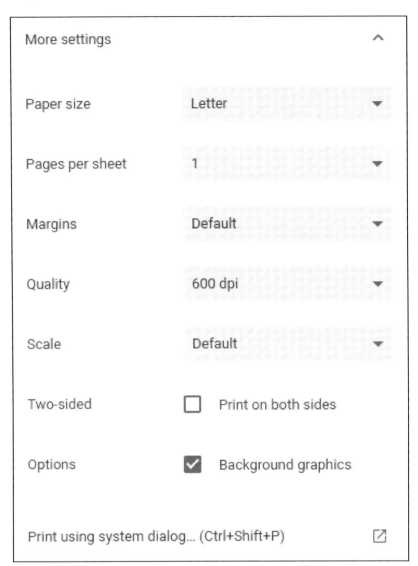

Figure 3.50

The last item under More settings is the *Print using system dialog* option. You might have noticed that printing with Docs doesn't look the same as when you print from your other programs such as Microsoft Word for example. This is because Docs is a web based application and uses its own printing processes.

If you want to use the Windows print process (assuming you are using Windows) because you are used to it then you can click on this option. You will then be given the typical Windows print dialog settings (figure 3.51) where you can get into some more advanced printer settings based on the make and model of your printer.

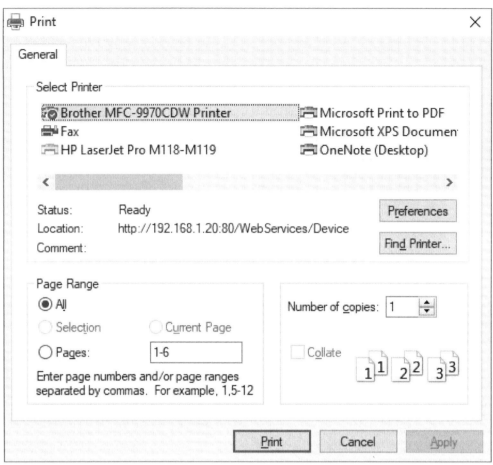

Figure 3.51

Chapter 4 – Document Formatting

Now that you know how to add things such as text, images and tables to your document, it's time to spruce it up a bit to make it more presentable for your readers. You don't need to wait until you are finished with your document to start formatting it but just make sure that everything is formatted uniformly when you are finished so it has a consistent look to it.

Proper formatting will also help make your document more readable and easier to navigate assuming you have formatted things properly. If you have a bunch of different size text, use multiple fonts and colors then things might start to look a little messy.

Formatting Text

I would like to begin this chapter with some text formatting tips. Formatting your text is easy to do but is one of the biggest factors in how your overall document looks.

Figure 4.1 shows some text along with an image that is used as an illustration for the subject matter. As you can see, all the text kind of blends together and the other real thing keeping things semi organized are the breaks from the paragraphs.

I will now apply some text and paragraph alignment formatting to make things look a bit better and easier to read. The key is knowing when to stop formatting so you don't end up overdoing it and making your document look like it was hit by a graffiti tagger!

Moving, Copying, Renaming and Deleting Files

One thing you will be doing a lot of once you are more comfortable with your file management skills will be copying, moving, renaming, and deleting files as needed. But before we begin our discussion, I must say BE CAREFUL when doing so to files, because you can cause your programs or even cause Windows to stop working if you play around with the wrong files. And, of course, you can also misplace or delete your own personal files, which is never a good thing.

Manipulating file locations is very common because you have so many options as to what you can do with your files and where you can store them. This all applies to folders as well by the way, so keep that in mind. If you are working on a document, for example, and want to save it, then you can pretty much save it wherever you want on your hard drive, even someplace you shouldn't like the Windows folder. So, what do you do if you need to move a file that you saved someplace you didn't want to save it at? The answer is easy. You move it! I will now go over three ways that you can move a file from one folder to another.

The first thing you need to do is to locate the file you want to move, and that can be done with Windows\File Explorer. Once you've found the file, simply click on it once to highlight it, and then you can go to the Home tab (figure 1), click on Move to, then choose a suggested location from the list or click on Choose Location at the bottom and browse to where you want to move the file to. It will then move the file. If you change your mind or picked the wrong folder, simply use the keyboard Ctrl-z shortcut to undo the last move.

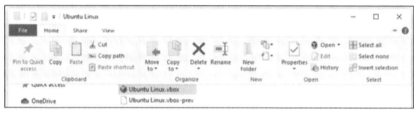

Figure 1

Another method you can use to move a file is to right click on it and choose Cut, then browse to the folder you want to move it to, right click on a blank area, and choose Paste. Just be careful not to choose Paste shortcut, because that is not the same thing, and I will be discussing what that is later in the chapter. The last method you can use involves the keyboard shortcuts you learned earlier in the chapter. Once you have

Figure 4.1

Figure 4.2 shows the results after some simple text formatting and here is what I did to accomplish that.

- Changed the font for all of the text
- Changed the first line to Header text
- Changed the text color on *BE CAREFUL* to red and made it bold
- Made the text that says *Windows\File Explorer* Bold
- Made the *Figure 1* text italicized
- Enlarged the image so it fit with the width of the text
- Changed the paragraph alignment to justified

Moving, Copying, Renaming and Deleting Files

One thing you will be doing a lot of once you are more comfortable with your file management skills will be copying, moving, renaming, and deleting files as needed. But before we begin our discussion, I must say **BE CAREFUL** when doing so to files, because you can cause your programs or even cause Windows to stop working if you play around with the wrong files. And, of course, you can also misplace or delete your own personal files, which is never a good thing.

Manipulating file locations is very common because you have so many options as to what you can do with your files and where you can store them. This all applies to folders as well by the way, so keep that in mind. If you are working on a document, for example, and want to save it, then you can pretty much save it wherever you want on your hard drive, even someplace you shouldn't like the Windows folder. So, what do you do if you need to move a file that you saved someplace you didn't want to save it at? The answer is easy. You move it! I will now go over three ways that you can move a file from one folder to another.

The first thing you need to do is to locate the file you want to move, and that can be done with **Windows\File Explorer**. Once you've found the file, simply click on it once to highlight it, and then you can go to the Home tab (*figure 1*), click on Move to, then choose a suggested location from the list or click on Choose Location at the bottom and browse to where you want to move the file to. It will then move the file. If you change your mind or picked the wrong folder, simply use the keyboard Ctrl-z shortcut to undo the last move.

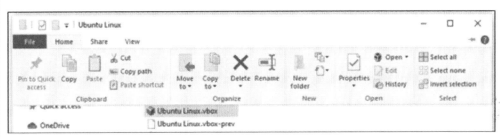

Figure 1

Another method you can use to move a file is to right click on it and choose Cut, then browse to the folder you want to move it to, right click on a blank area, and choose Paste. Just be careful not to choose Paste shortcut, because that is not the same thing, and I will

Figure 4.2

As you can see, it doesn't take too much work to make your document more presentable by only changing a few things. And the best part is, if you make a change and don't like it, you don't have to keep it!

Adding Additional Fonts

You might have noticed that Docs only comes with a limited number of fonts that you can use in your documents. If you are used to using other programs that are installed on your computer, you might have noticed that you have many more fonts to choose from. This is because most programs installed on your computer will use the fonts that are installed on your operating system (Windows, Mac OS etc.) and many programs will add additional fonts to your computer when you install them. Plus you can buy or download hundreds or thousands of additional fonts to be used on your computer if you desire.

Since Docs is a web based application, you are stuck with whatever fonts come with the app. Fortunately, there is a way to add additional fonts to Docs so you will have some more options when it comes to formatting your text.

To add these additional fonts you will need to go to the font section on the toolbar and then click on *More fonts* at the top of your font list as seen in figure 4.3.

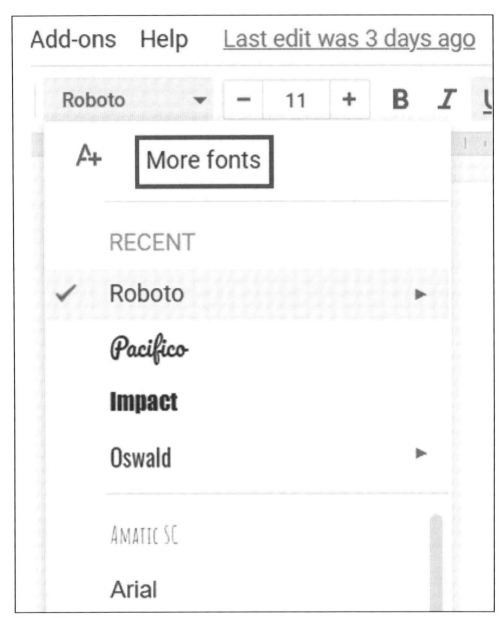

Figure 4.3

Next you will be presented with a list of fonts that you can add to Docs and all you need to do is put a checkmark next to the fonts you would like to add and then click the *OK* button and they will automatically be added to Docs for you to be able to use.

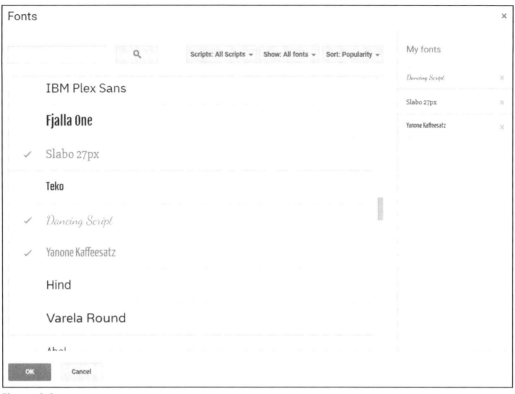

Figure 4.4

Editing Images Within Your Document

If you plan on adding images to your documents, it's always a good idea to have these images looking the way you want them to look before inserting them into your document. But sometimes you will be inserting images right from Docs as I discussed in the last chapter and won't have a chance to edit them beforehand.

Fortunately, you can do some basic image editing within docs if you would like to try and enhance your pictures a bit to make them look a little better. Once you have your image in place you can click on it to highlight it and then you will have a few options as seen in figure 4.5

Figure 4.5

If you click on *All image options* you will be shown all of the image editing choices. I will now go over what each one of these editing options will do.

Size & Rotation
If you need to shrink or enlarge your image you would normally do so by dragging a corner with the mouse until it looks the way want. But if you need to have your image be a specific size then you can manually type in the width and height or change the scale percentage by typing in a number or using the up and down arrows. The *Lock aspect ratio* checkbox will make sure that the scaling of your image stays correct so you don't end up stretching it out by enlarging the width but not the height for example.

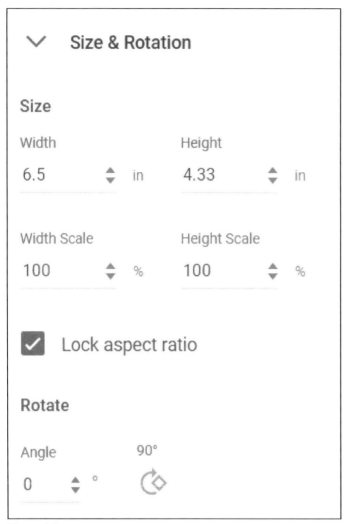

Figure 4.6

If you need to rotate your image you can type the angle (in degrees) in the box or use the up and down arrows to rotate your image one degree at a time. If you know you need to rotate your image 90 degrees you can click on the 90° button to do it in one step.

Text Wrapping
If you have text that applies to your image and don't want to just have your text be above or below your picture (inline), then you can apply some text wrapping to give your document more of a brochure type appearance. The *Wrap text* option will put your text around all four sides of the image (unless you specify otherwise), essentially wrapping your image with text.

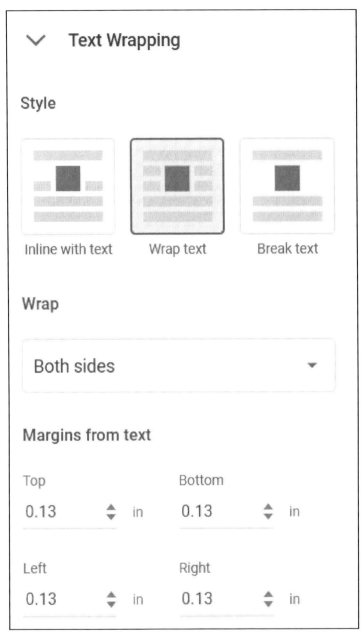

Figure 4.7

The *Break text* option, your text will stay above and below the image, breaking up the text into which you inserted it.

Position
Normally when you have text above your picture and then add more text or press Enter on your keyboard, your image will move down the page along with the text.

If you do not want it to move with the text but rather have the text move below the image as you type or add new lines then you can use the *Fix position on page* option.

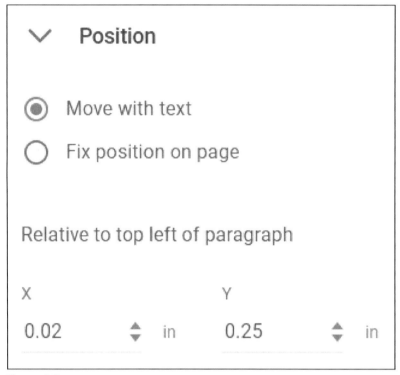

Figure 4.8

 If your image is on the default setting of inline with text then you will notice that the Position option is greyed out. This is because the Position settings apply only to images that use the *wrap text* or *break text* setting. The *Inline with text* option treats your image like text so it moves along with your text as you type.

Recolor

This adjustment option will apply a colored filter to your image and pretty much remove all the different colors that might be in your original image. There are several color shades to choose from such as red, blue, yellow and so on.

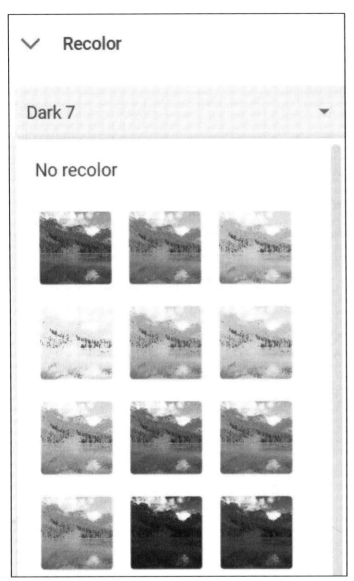

Figure 4.9

Adjustments

There are three basic image adjustments you can make from this area. If you would like to add some transparency (see-through) to your image then you can move the slider to the right or left to adjust that attribute. If you need to adjust the brightness or contrast of your image you can do so with the corresponding sliders.

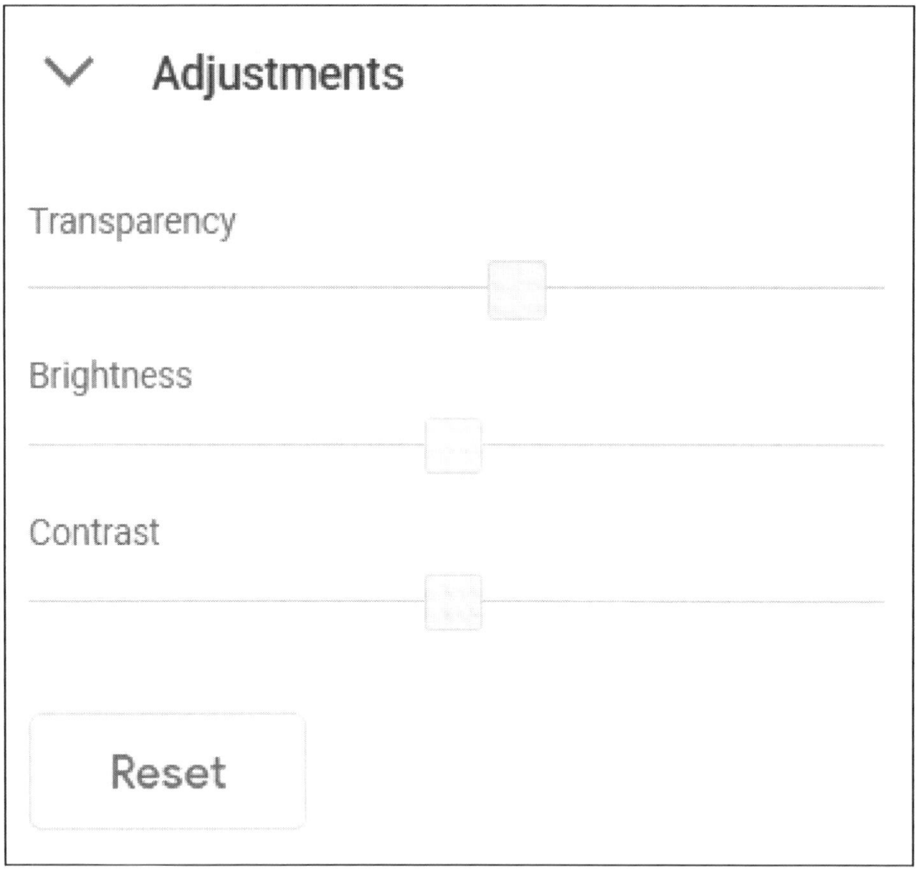

Figure 4.10

Page Setup

In addition to formatting the contents on your page, you also need to format the page itself, especially if you plan on printing your document. There aren't too many page setup options in Docs compared to other programs like Microsoft Word, but the available options should still be enough to get your document looking good on the screen and on paper when you print it out.

To get to the page setup options simply go to the *File* menu and then click on *Page setup*. As you can see in figure 4.11, you have four attributes that you can change.

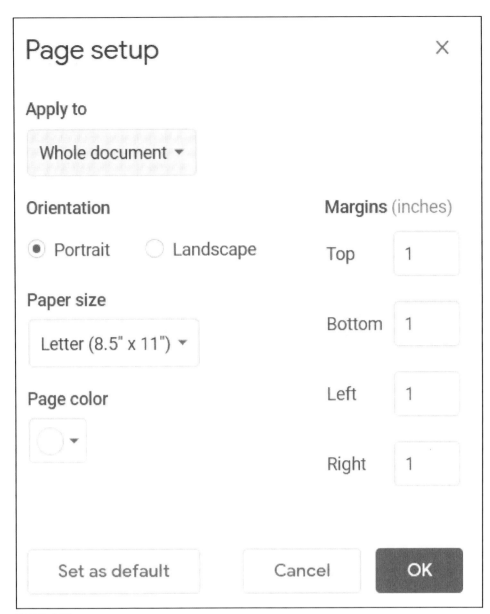

Figure 4.11

- **Orientation** - lets you choose if you want your page to be tall or wide. Most of the time you will use portrait but there may be times you need to use landscape if you have wide pictures or tables for example.

- **Paper size** – Docs has many commonly used paper sizes to choose from such as letter and legal but unfortunately you can't enter in custom paper sizes without using some type of add-on application such as *Paper Sizer* which I will be discussing in Chapter 7.

101

- **Page color** – If you would like to add a background color to your page then you can set that from here. Just make sure you can still read the text after applying the color to your pages otherwise you will need to change your text color.

 Everyone knows how expensive printer ink is, so if you plan on using colored backgrounds for your documents you might end up running out of ink sooner than expected. You might want to try colored paper instead! You can also use the "draft" option from your printer properties to save one ink when printing.

- **Margins** – The page margins specify how much "white space" you have from the edge of the page to where your text starts. Just make sure your margins are not so small that your printer cuts off your text because it can't support such small margins.

The *Apply to* setting will let you set specific margins to a certain section of your document. So if you highlight that section first and then go to the page setup you can set margins just for that selected content or that section if you have section breaks (figure 4.12). You will not be able to change things like page color and size just for a section though.

Deleting files is pretty straightforward, and all you have to do is highlight the file and click the Delete button from figure 3.28. Or you can right click a file and choose Delete or press the Delete key on your keyboard. By default, Windows will send the file to the Recycle Bin rather than delete them permanently. If you made a mistake and want the file back, you can use Ctrl-z for undo to have the file undeleted from the Recycle Bin and retur... ...last operation, so if you deleted anot... ...have to go into the Recycle Bin t...

If you want to see all... ...ktop, or, if for some reason you don... ...n the Windows\File Explore... ...system files option unchecked.

Once you are in the R... ...name, size, original location, date... ...simply right click on it and choose... ...This will move the file back to its ori... ...aste it wherever you like or simply dra...

If you right click the R... ...polbar, you will see its location and h...

Page setup

×

Apply to

This section (Section 3) ▾

Orientation

● Portrait   Landscape

Paper size

Letter, 8.5 x 1... ▾

Page color

Margins (inches)

Top   1

Bottom   1

Left   1

Right   1

Set as default   Cancel   **OK**

Figure 4.12

The *Set as default* option will keep whatever settings you make here as your defaults for new documents in the future.

Paragraph Styles

Paragraph styles are used to apply text formatting such as title text or header text to parts of your document. These styles can help you organize your outlines and are also used when creating a table of contents for your work. To use a particular style, highlight the text you want that style to apply to and then go to the *Format* menu, *Paragraph styles* and then choose the style you want from the list. Title text will be larger than subtitle text and Heading 1 text will be larger than Heading 2 text and so on. You should just play around with these to get a feel of how each one will look.

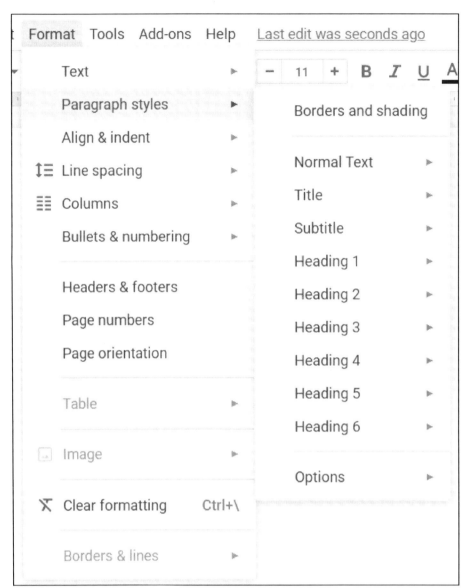

Figure 4.13

Figure 4.14 shows what happens after I applied some title and header text to my document and then clicked on the *show document outline* button at the top right of the screen (outlines will be discussed later in this chapter). If I didn't have these styles applied then I wouldn't have anything shown for my outline. If you use the *Update 'Heading X' to match* selection then all of the text in your document with the same text type, such as Heading 2 or subtitle, will be updated to match your initial selection.

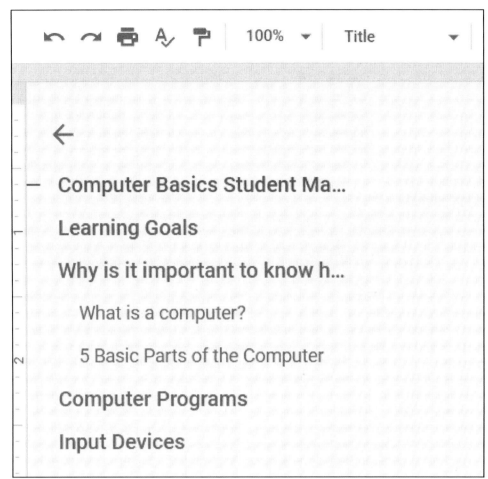

Figure 4.14

You can also apply some borders and shading to a paragraph by highlighting the paragraph and then choosing the *Borders and shading* option. Here I can have Docs but a border around whichever side of the paragraph I choose, and I can also have it fill in that paragraph with a background color. Figure 4.15 shows that I want to add a top and bottom border with a 3 pt. line thickness. I also chose red for the border color and yellow for the background color. Figure 4.16 shows the results after I click on the *Apply* button.

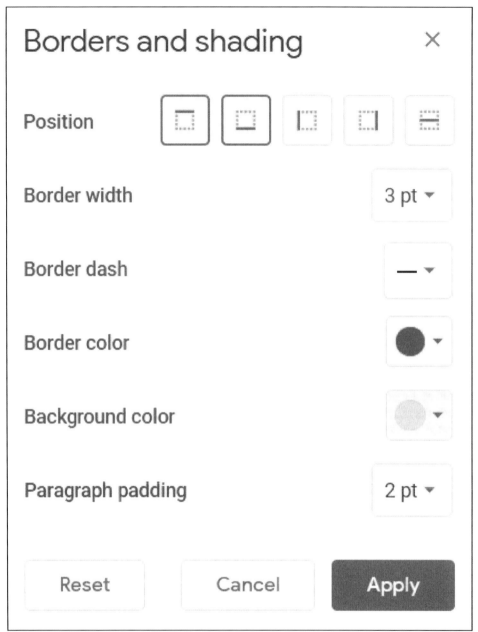

Figure 4.15

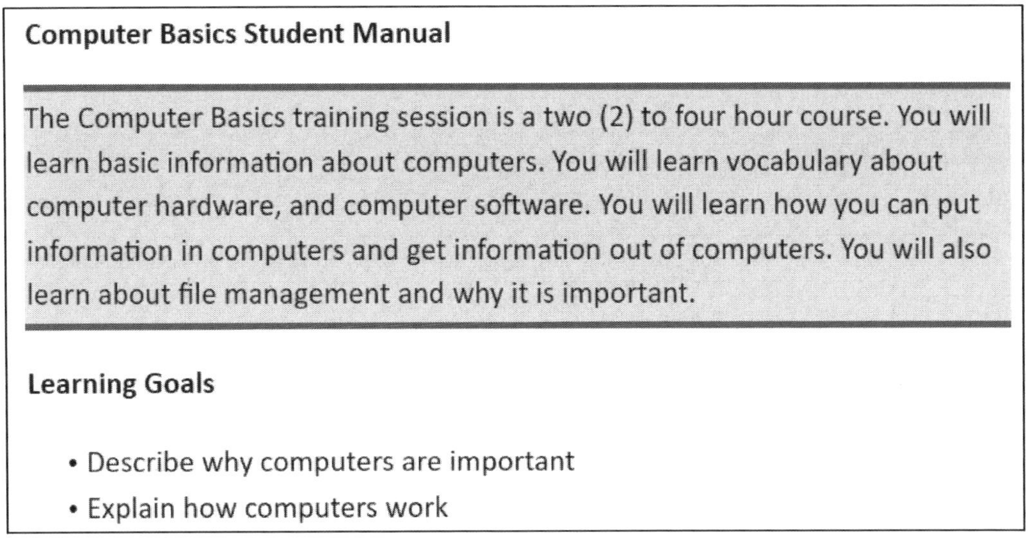

Computer Basics Student Manual

The Computer Basics training session is a two (2) to four hour course. You will learn basic information about computers. You will learn vocabulary about computer hardware, and computer software. You will learn how you can put information in computers and get information out of computers. You will also learn about file management and why it is important.

Learning Goals

- Describe why computers are important
- Explain how computers work

Figure 4.16

Paint Format Tool

One tool that you might find useful to help speed up the formatting process is the Paint format tool. This is used to apply formatting from one area to another with just a click of the mouse. Let's say I had some text that uses a certain font, font size, and was also bold and I wanted to apply all three of those attributes to some other text to make it match without having to go figure out what exactly I need to change. Figure 4.17 shows the text with the formatting that I want to apply to the text in figure 4.18.

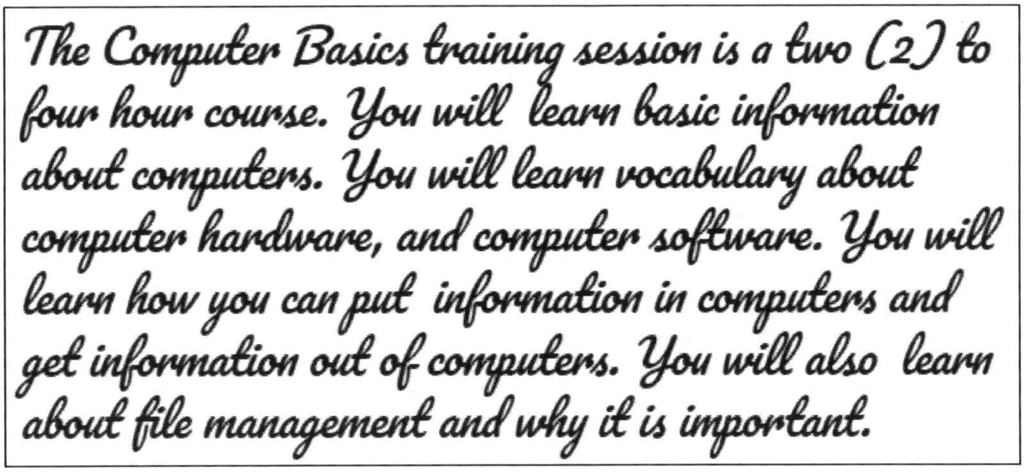

The Computer Basics training session is a two (2) to four hour course. You will learn basic information about computers. You will learn vocabulary about computer hardware, and computer software. You will learn how you can put information in computers and get information out of computers. You will also learn about file management and why it is important.

Figure 4.17

Computers are everywhere and everyone is using them! Computers are in our cars, our kitchens, our stores and in our workplaces. They are used to communicate, to play, and to make everyday tasks easier. Using a computer and the Internet will help you to keep in touch with friends and family.

Figure 4.18

To make the formatting match all I need to do is highlight the text in figure 4.17, then click on the Paint format tool so it's highlighted in blue (figure 4.19)

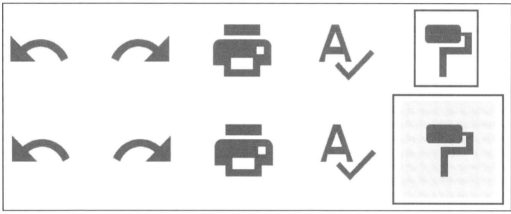

Figure 4.19

Then once I highlight the text from figure 4.18 and let go of the mouse, the formatting will apply, and it will look like the text in figure 4.20

Computers are everywhere and everyone is using them! Computers are in our cars, our kitchens, our stores and in our workplaces. They are used to communicate, to play, and to make everyday tasks easier. Using a computer and the Internet will help you to keep in touch with friends and family.

Figure 4.20

Creating Lists

Lists are another way to format your text to make it easier to follow or understand. If you have a listing of individual items, putting them in a list will make a huge difference in how easy your document is to follow.

Take the text from figure 4.21 for example. It's not very easy to follow and you might find yourself having to re-read it to make sure you followed the steps in order.

Here are the required steps you should take to install our new software on your computer. Turn on the computer. Put the installation DVD into your drive. When the autorun menu comes up, click on install. Then you will need to choose your installation directory. Put in your serial number when asked. Then click on the Install button to start the installation process. When it's complete you can then click on the Finish button. Then reboot your computer and you can start using the software.

Figure 4.21

Now look at the same information formatted with a bulleted list (figure 4.22). I was even able to shorten some of the sentences when formatting the instructions this way.

Here are the required steps you should take to install our new software on your computer.

- Turn on the computer
- Put the installation DVD into your drive
- When the autorun menu comes up, click on install
- Choose your installation directory
- Put in your serial number when asked
- Click on the Install button to start the installation process
- When it's complete you can then click on the Finish button
- Reboot your computer and you can start using the software

Figure 4.22

I can even use the numbered list option if that works better for me.

Here are the required steps you should take to install our new software on your computer.

1. Turn on the computer
2. Put the installation DVD into your drive
3. When the autorun menu comes up, click on install
4. Choose your installation directory
5. Put in your serial number when asked
6. Click on the Install button to start the installation process
7. When it's complete you can then click on the Finish button
8. Reboot your computer and you can start using the software

Figure 4.23

To create a list, it's best to have each list item on its own line and then you can highlight all the lines of text and click on the bulleted list or numbered list icon on the toolbar.

Figure 4.24

When using numbered or bulleted lists, you are not restricted to just a basic list but can actually have sub items in your lists if they need to be more complex. If you click on the down arrows next to each type of list you will see that you have options as to how your bullets or numbers are formatted for sub topics on your list (figures 4.25 & 4.26).

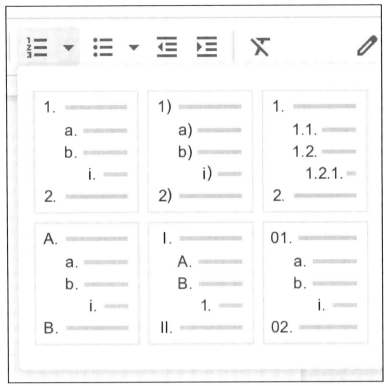

Figure 4.25

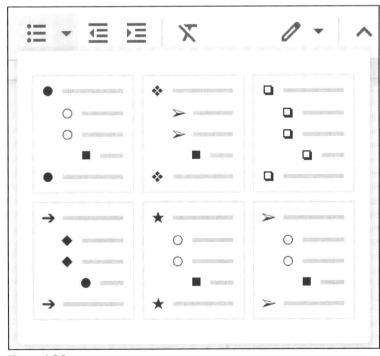

Figure 4.26

To add sub items to your list you can type the text on the next line and then press the Tab key on your keyboard and Docs will automatically make it a sub item as seen in figure 4.27.

Here are the required steps you should take to install our new software on your computer.

1. Turn on the computer
   a. Push the power button
2. Put the installation DVD into your drive
3. When the autorun menu comes up, click on install
   a. If it doesn't start automatically, click on setup.exe
4. Choose your installation directory
5. Put in your serial number when asked
   a. This is on the back of the box
      i. You can also get it online from your account
6. Click on the Install button to start the installation process
7. When it's complete you can then click on the Finish button
8. Reboot your computer and you can start using the software
   a. Be sure to save any open files first

Figure 4.27

Headers & Footers

When creating documents you might find the need to add additional information on each page such as a chapter title or document revision number and this is where headers and footers can really help you out. Headers consist of text at the top of each page and footers are found at the bottom of each pager. If you are reading the paperback version of this book you will see the chapter name at the top of the page. This is an example of a header.

To create a header in Docs you will need to go to the *Insert* menu and then click on *Headers & footers* and then click on *Headers*. Now you will be able to type in your header text at the top of the page (figure 4.28). Just make sure it's not too long because it will look out of place if you do. When you are finished typing, simply click off the page and your header will be in place on each page (figure 4.29).

Figure 4.28

Figure 4.29

The checkbox for *Different first page* is used if you would like to have a different header for the first page compared to the headers used on the rest of your pages.

Clicking on *Options* will give you a way to increase or decrease the margin of the header text from the top of the page. You can also set the different first page option from here and configure different headers for odd and even pages.

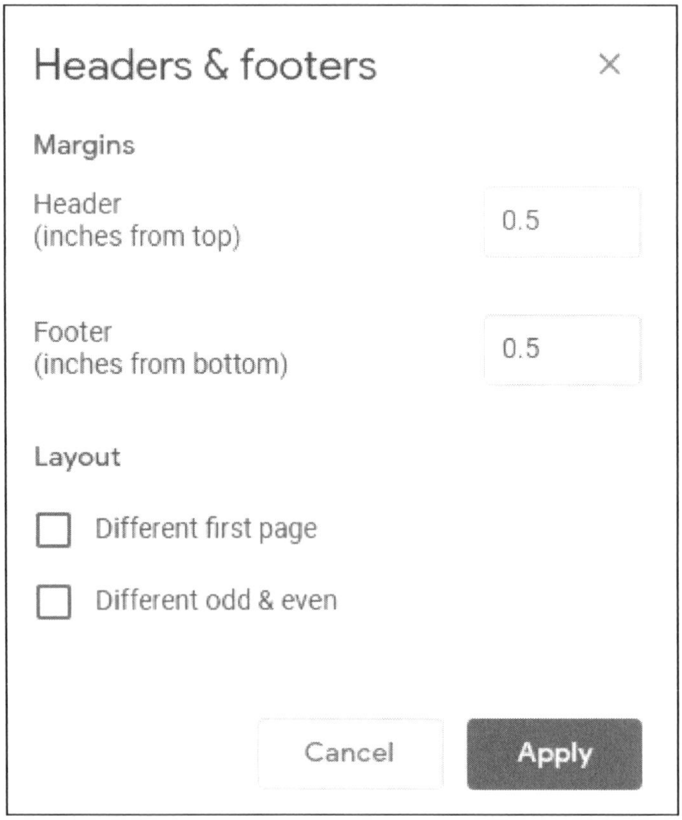

Headers & footers ✕

Margins

Header
(inches from top)   0.5

Footer
(inches from bottom)   0.5

Layout

☐ Different first page

☐ Different odd & even

Cancel   Apply

Figure 4.30

Footers work the same way as headers do but you also have the option to add page numbers to your document from the footer options. I will be discussing page numbers next.

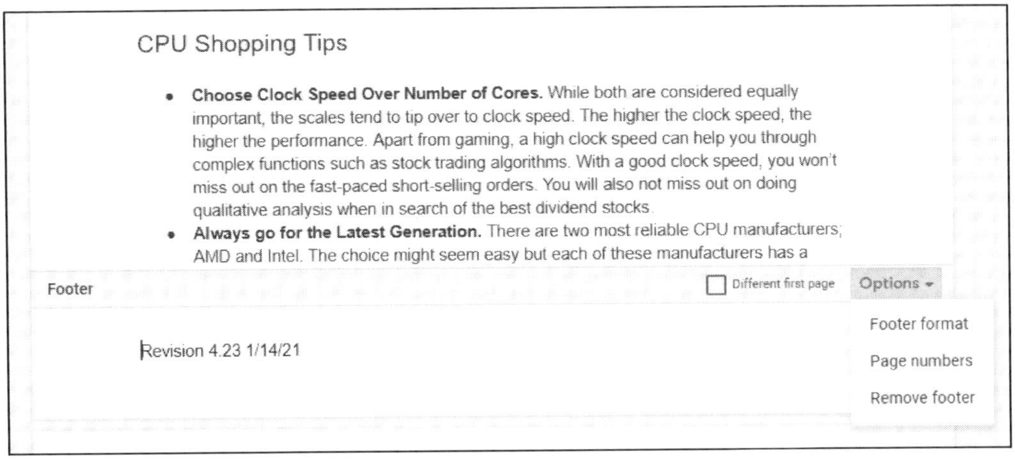

Figure 4.31

Page Numbers

Page numbers are another type of footer that you can add to your document in case you want to have all of your pages numbered. If you are planning on adding a table of contents to your document then you will need to have your pages numbered otherwise it doesn't do you much good.

When you click on *Insert* and then *Page numbers* you will be given some default choices as to where you would like your page numbers to be inserted such as the top right of the page on every other page etc.

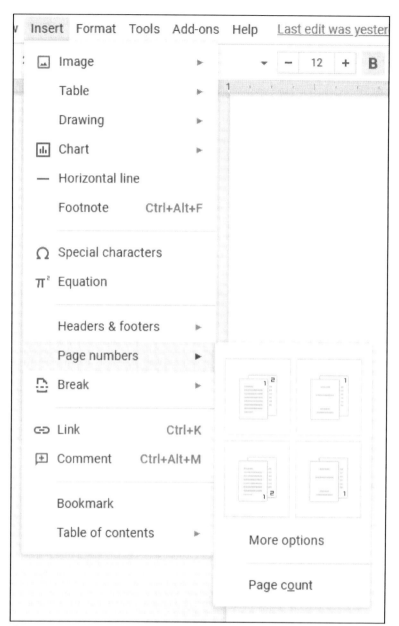

Figure 4.32

Clicking on *More options* will give you some additional choices as to how the page numbers will be applied to your document. From here you can choose whether the page number is at the top of the page (header) or bottom of the page (footer) and also whether or not the first page will be numbered. You can also have your page numbers start from a different number than one by entering that number in the *Start at* box.

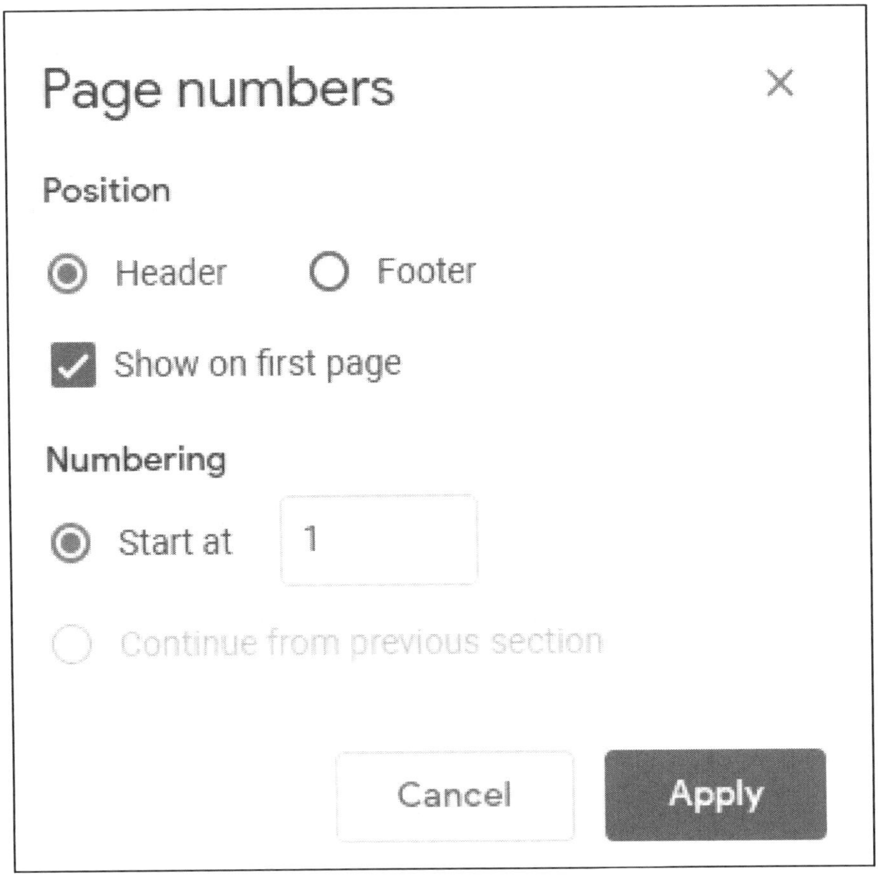

Page numbers ✕

Position

◉ Header   ○ Footer

☑ Show on first page

Numbering

◉ Start at   [1]

○ Continue from previous section

[Cancel]   [**Apply**]

Figure 4.33

As you type and add pages, Docs will increment the page number to go along with the number of pages you have for your document, so you don't need to worry about adding page numbers again later if you add more pages.

Indenting Text

Docs will let you indent sentences and paragraphs within your document if you like to do things such as indent the first line of your paragraphs or have a paragraph appear as a sub topic of another paragraph. To indent your text you can either use the Indent buttons on the toolbar (figure 4.34) or the *Format>Align & indent* menu selection.

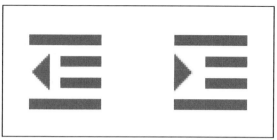

Figure 4.34

Figure 4.35 shows an example of a first line indent and then I also indented my numbered list quite a bit just to show you how indentation can look.

> Here are the required steps you should take to install our new software on your computer. Turn on the computer. Put the installation DVD into your drive. When the autorun menu comes up, click on install. Then you will need to choose your installation directory. Put in your serial number when asked. Then click on the Install button to start the installation process. When it's complete you can then click on the Finish button. Then reboot your computer and you can start using the software.
>
> Here are the required steps you should take to install our new software on your computer.
>
> 1. Turn on the computer
> 2. Put the installation DVD into your drive
> 3. When the autorun menu comes up, click on install
> 4. Choose your installation directory
> 5. Put in your serial number when asked
> 6. Click on the Install button to start the installation process
> 7. When it's complete you can then click on the Finish button
> 8. Reboot your computer and you can start using the software

Figure 4.35

To perform a first line indent you will need to go to the indentation options as seen in figure 4.36 and then choose *First line* under *Special indent*.

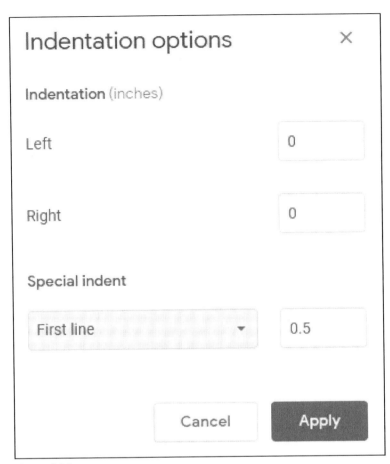

Figure 4.36

You can also use the ruler to perform indentations with your text by sliding the blue markers on the ruler that indicate where the left, right, first line indents etc. are located. In figure 4.37 the mouse cursor is placed at the front of the word Here in the first sentence. When I place the mouse here, the marker on the ruler will reflect where my mouse cursor is. In this case it's at the first line indent. If I were to move my cursor in front of the first item in my numbered list, then it would put the marker on the ruler there instead (figure 4.38).

Here are the required steps you should take to install our new software on your computer. Turn on the computer. Put the installation DVD into your drive. When the autorun menu comes up, click on install. Then you will need to choose your installation directory. Put in your serial number when asked. Then click on the Install button to start the installation process. When it's complete you can then click on the Finish button. Then reboot your computer and you can start using the software.

Here are the required steps you should take to install our new software on your computer.

1. Turn on the computer
2. Put the installation DVD into your drive
3. When the autorun menu comes up, click on install
4. Choose your installation directory
5. Put in your serial number when asked
6. Click on the Install button to start the installation process
7. When it's complete you can then click on the Finish button
8. Reboot your computer and you can start using the software

Figure 4.37

Here are the required steps you should take to install our new software on your computer. Turn on the computer. Put the installation DVD into your drive. When the autorun menu comes up, click on install. Then you will need to choose your installation directory. Put in your serial number when asked. Then click on the Install button to start the installation process. When it's complete you can then click on the Finish button. Then reboot your computer and you can start using the software.

Here are the required steps you should take to install our new software on your computer.

1. Turn on the computer
2. Put the installation DVD into your drive
3. When the autorun menu comes up, click on install
4. Choose your installation directory
5. Put in your serial number when asked
6. Click on the Install button to start the installation process
7. When it's complete you can then click on the Finish button
8. Reboot your computer and you can start using the software

Figure 4.38

If I were to slide the first line indent marker over to the 2 inch spot on the ruler, my text would move over to line up at the 2 inch mark as well.

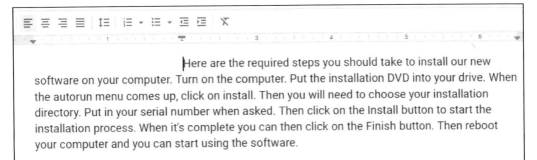

Figure 4.39

The key to using the ruler to indent your text is to make sure that you have your cursor in the right spot, otherwise you will be moving text that you probably didn't want to move.

Document Outline

When working on a document, it's nice to have a way to check the structure of your work to help you organize your content. Outlines use the text\paragraph styles to construct the outline. So if you use title or header text in your document then that will be used to create your document outline.

Figure 4.40 shows a document with basic formatting that is not using any text styles. Figure 4.41 shows the document after applying title and header styles to the main categories of the document. I also applied header 1, 2, 3 and header 4 styles to some other sub sections that are not shown.

Computer Programs

A computer program is a set of step-by-step instructions. These instructions tell the computer how to do its job.

Operating System Software

This software works with the operating system. It controls how you, the software, and the hardware work together. Windows, Apple, Android, and Chrome are common operating systems. Computers and laptops usually use Windows or Apple. Cell phones and tablets usually use Apple, Android, or Chrome software.

Application Software

This software is what the computer uses to carry out a job as specified by the user. There are different kinds of application software.

Office Productivity Software

Word Processing is software that lets you work mostly with text. You can enter, edit, format and print documents. Microsoft Word is a popular example of word processing software.

Spreadsheet software

Spreadsheet software helps you work with numbers and text too. You can enter, edit, format, print, sort and do math with spreadsheet software. Microsoft Excel is a popular example of spreadsheet software.

Communications Software

Communications software helps you read, write, talk to, and listen to other people. Examples are the Internet and Email. Internet Explore and Chrome are examples of Internet browsers. Browsers help you use the Internet.

Educational Software

These are computer applications that help people learn.

Entertainment

Entertainment applications are popular. Many people use applications to listen to music or books. They also use these entertainment applications to play games and watch movies.

Input Devices

Mouse

The mouse lets you work with text and objects on the computer screen. You use the mouse to:
- Double Click
- Right Click
- Click and Drag
- Drag and Drop

1.0.2 Mouse Practice is completed on the computer using the Mouse Practice file. |

Figure 4.40

Computer Programs

A computer program is a set of step-by-step instructions. These instructions tell the computer how to do its job.

Operating System Software

This software works with the operating system. It controls how you, the software, and the hardware work together. Windows, Apple, Android, and Chrome are common operating systems. Computers and laptops usually use Windows or Apple. Cell phones and tablets usually use Apple, Android, or Chrome software.

Application Software

This software is what the computer uses to carry out a job as specified by the user. There are different kinds of application software.

Office Productivity Software

Word Processing is software that lets you work mostly with text. You can enter, edit, format and print documents. Microsoft Word is a popular example of word processing software.

Spreadsheet software

Spreadsheet software helps you work with numbers and text too. You can enter, edit, format, print, sort and do math with spreadsheet software. Microsoft Excel is a popular example of spreadsheet software.

Communications Software

Communications software helps you read, write, talk to, and listen to other people. Examples are the Internet and Email. Internet Explorer and Chrome are examples of Internet browsers. Browsers help you use the Internet.

Figure 4.41

Figure 4.42 shows my outline now that I have the proper text styles applied to my document. You can see your outline by clicking on the *show document outline* icon at the top left of the screen.

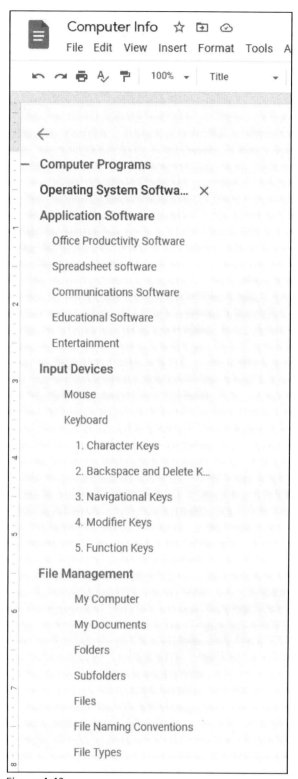

Figure 4.42

Adding a Table of Contents

If you are using docs to write a book or longer essay type paper then you probably want to add a table of contents so that your readers can navigate the contents of your work without having to flip through a bunch of pages searching for what they are looking for.

In order to add a table of contents in your Docs document you will need to use the proper type of heading text, so your sections make sense and are formatted correctly to be used for a table of contents. Then you can go to the *Insert* menu and choose *Table of contents* and decide if you want to use a table of contents with page numbers or with links that can be clicked on to take you to a specific page.

The *with page numbers* option is best for when you are printing your document since you obviously can't click on links on a printed copy. If you are planning on sharing your document or emailing it to people and want them to be able to click on a part of your table of contents to go to a specific page then you can use the *with blue links* option.

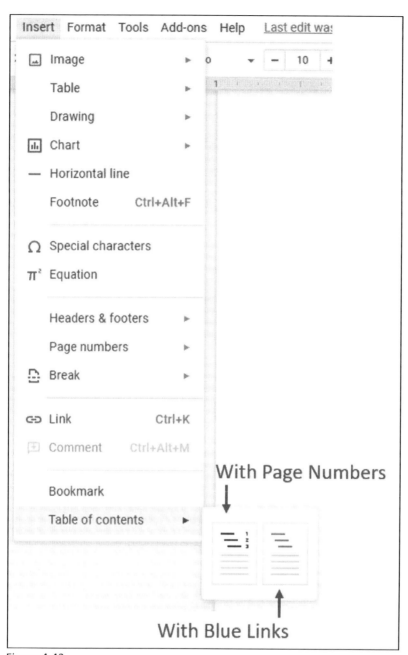

Figure 4.43

I have opened one of my books in Docs and formatted the chapter and section text for the first four chapters using the header 1 and header 2 styles and figure 4.44 shows the results when I create a table of contents using the with page numbers style.

Introduction	**2**
Chapter 1 – What is Google Classroom?	**3**
Intended Users	4
G-suite for Education	5
Google Classroom Interface	8
Chapter 2 – Accessing Google Classroom	**10**
Signing Up for a Google Account	10
Signing into Google Classroom	12
Teacher vs. Student Views	13
Chapter 3 – Creating a Class	**15**
Adding a Class	15
Class Settings	17
Customizing the Look of Your Class	18
Copying a Class	20
Adding Students to Your Class	23
Removing Students and Leaving Classes	26
Inviting Other Teachers to Your Class	27
Classroom Guardians	28
Organizing Your Class Cards	29
Archiving and Deleting Classes	30
Chapter 4 – Running Your Classes	**32**
Stream Tab	32
Stream Tab Attachments	36
Adding Assignments, Materials and Quizzes Using the Classwork Tab	39
Topics	49
People Tab	51
To Review and To-do Sections	53
Class Drive Folder	55

Figure 4.44

Figure 4.45 shows the results if I choose the with blue links option. If you look at ether version of the table of contents I created you will notice a circular arrow icon at the top right, next to the word Introduction. This is a refresh option so if you make changes in your document and move stuff around, you can click on this refresh button to have your TOC updated. This icon will not print and will go away when you click off your TOC by the way.

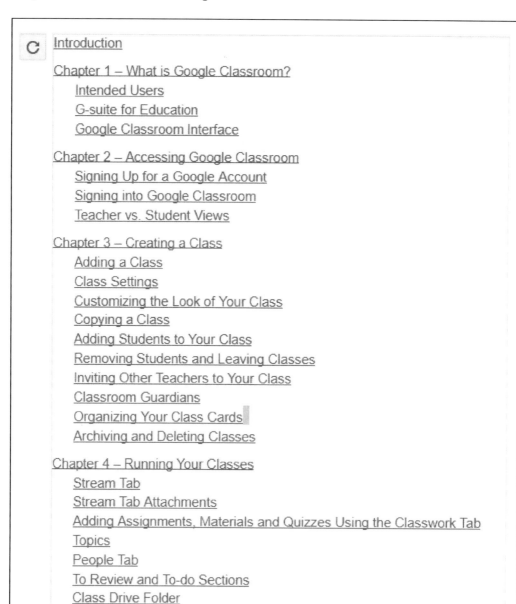

Figure 4.45

Checking Your Spelling and Grammar

We all know that nobody is perfect and that's especially true when it comes to our typing and spelling skills! You should know by now that when you see the squiggly red line under a word in your document that it means you spelled that word incorrectly. And when you see the squiggly blue line it means there is some type of grammar error.

When you are working on your document you can fix any spelling and grammar errors as you go but many people like to wait until they are finished with their document and take care of it all at once. Either way works perfectly fine so it's up to you how you want to go about it.

Figure 4.46 shows a few paragraphs that have some spelling and grammar errors. If I want to fix my errors as I go along I can either fix the text itself or I can right click on them one at a time and see if one of the spelling or grammar suggestions is the one I want and then apply that fix by clicking on the appropriate one.

Figure 4.47 shows what happens when I right click on a spelling error and figure 4.48 shows what happens with a grammar error. You might just get one suggestion but if your spelling or grammar is really bad you might get more than one because it will be harder for Docs to figure out what you really meant to type.

In todays changing environment we need to be able to adapt and change along with it in order to still be able to get the things done that we need to. This applies to both our work, home and learning enviroments and if we need to spend all of our time figurng out how to do our work then we will never get any of it done.

When it comes to online learning, it's important to have a system that is easy to use yet can utilize all of the functionality of a real life in person classroom such as assigning tasks to students, having interactive live meetings and testing them on what they have learned. Plus of course you also need a way to grade your students based on their performance.

Google Classroom has been around for some time now and is always being improved upon to make it easier to use and more capable as an online teaching and learning tool. With Classroom you can host various classes with specific students in each class and also have the same students in multiple classes. You can also prepare lesson plans assignments quizzes and other material specific to each one of your classes or share the content between some or all of your classes.

The goal of this book is to get you up and running with Google Classroom and show you how to create your classes, add students, distribute your learning materials and grade your student's performance. I will also show you how to join and participate in an class from a student's point of view so you can see how each side works. You will see that there are several ways to accomplish many of the typical tasks you will be performing so you will be able to find the way that works the best for you, or use sevral methods!

Figure 4.46

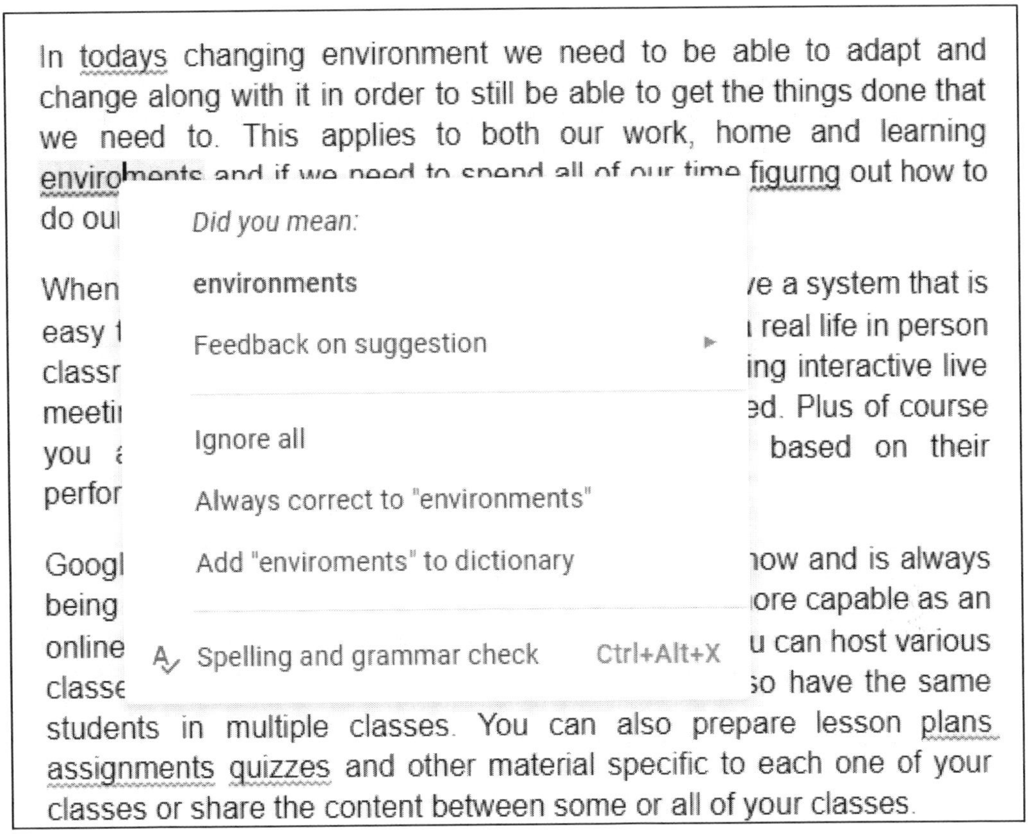

In todays changing environment we need to be able to adapt and change along with it in order to still be able to get the things done that we need to. This applies to both our work, home and learning enviro~~lments and if we need to spend all of our time~~ figurng out how to do ou

Did you mean:

environments

Feedback on suggestion ▸

Ignore all

Always correct to "environments"

Add "enviroments" to dictionary

A̬ Spelling and grammar check   Ctrl+Alt+X

When ... /e a system that is
easy ... real life in person
classr ... ing interactive live
meeti ... ed. Plus of course
you ... based on their
perfor

Googl ... ow and is always
being ... ore capable as an
online ... u can host various
classe ... so have the same
students in multiple classes. You can also prepare lesson plans, assignments quizzes and other material specific to each one of your classes or share the content between some or all of your classes.

Figure 4.47

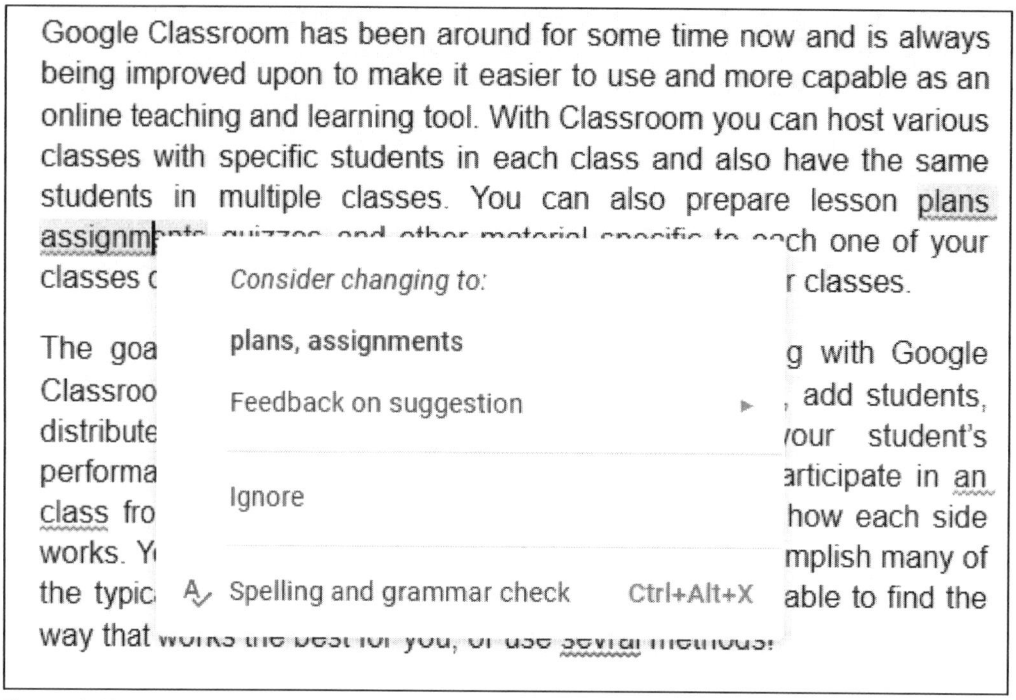

Google Classroom has been around for some time now and is always being improved upon to make it easier to use and more capable as an online teaching and learning tool. With Classroom you can host various classes with specific students in each class and also have the same students in multiple classes. You can also prepare lesson plans assignm~~ents quizzes and other material specific to each~~ one of your classes ~~classes d~~ r classes.

Consider changing to:

The goa plans, assignments g with Google
Classroo Feedback on suggestion ▸ , add students,
distribute our student's
performa artiicipate in an
class fro Ignore how each side
works. Y mplish many of
the typic A Spelling and grammar check Ctrl+Alt+X able to find the
way that ~~works the best for you, or use sevral methods!~~

Figure 4.48

You might have noticed some of the other options you have when you right click on a misspelled word or grammar error. If you disagree with Docs that your mistake is even a mistake then you can click on *Ignore* so the underline will go away yet you can keep your original text. The *add "your text" to dictionary* option will add your word, misspelled or not to the built in dictionary so it won't be flagged as misspelled from now on.

If you want to run the spelling and grammar checker on your entire document rather than right clicking on individual errors then you can go to the *Tools* menu and then click on *Spelling and grammar check*. If you take a look at figure 4.49 you will see that *Show spelling suggestions* and *Show grammar suggestions* are both checked. If you do not want to see the squiggly lines underneath your errors then you can uncheck one or both of these.

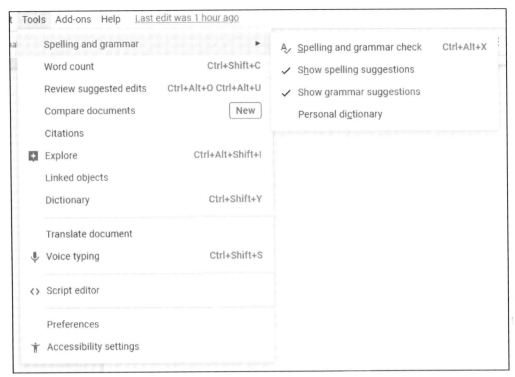

Figure 4.49

The Personal dictionary option will show you any words that you have added from the spell checker and you can also add additional words from here that you don't want to be marked as misspelled.

Personal dictionary   ×

Add a new word   Add

mispellled

                                              Cancel   OK

Figure 4.50

Once I click on Spelling and grammar check, Docs will go through my document and show me one potential error at a time, and I can either choose to accept its suggested correction or ignore it and move on. If I click on the three vertical dots next to the Accept button I will have the option to accept or ignore any instances of the misspelled word and also add it to my personal dictionary if I like (for spelling errors only).

Figure 4.51

The spelling and grammar checker will begin wherever your cursor is located in your document. So if you don't have your cursor at the beginning of the area you want it to start at, it will not cover everything you are hoping to have it check.

Word Count

If for some reason you need to know the statistics of your document in regards to how many words, characters, pages etc. that you have then you can see that very easily by going to the *Tools* menu and then clicking on *Word count*. This will open a window that shows you this information to give you a quick overview of how much work you have done.

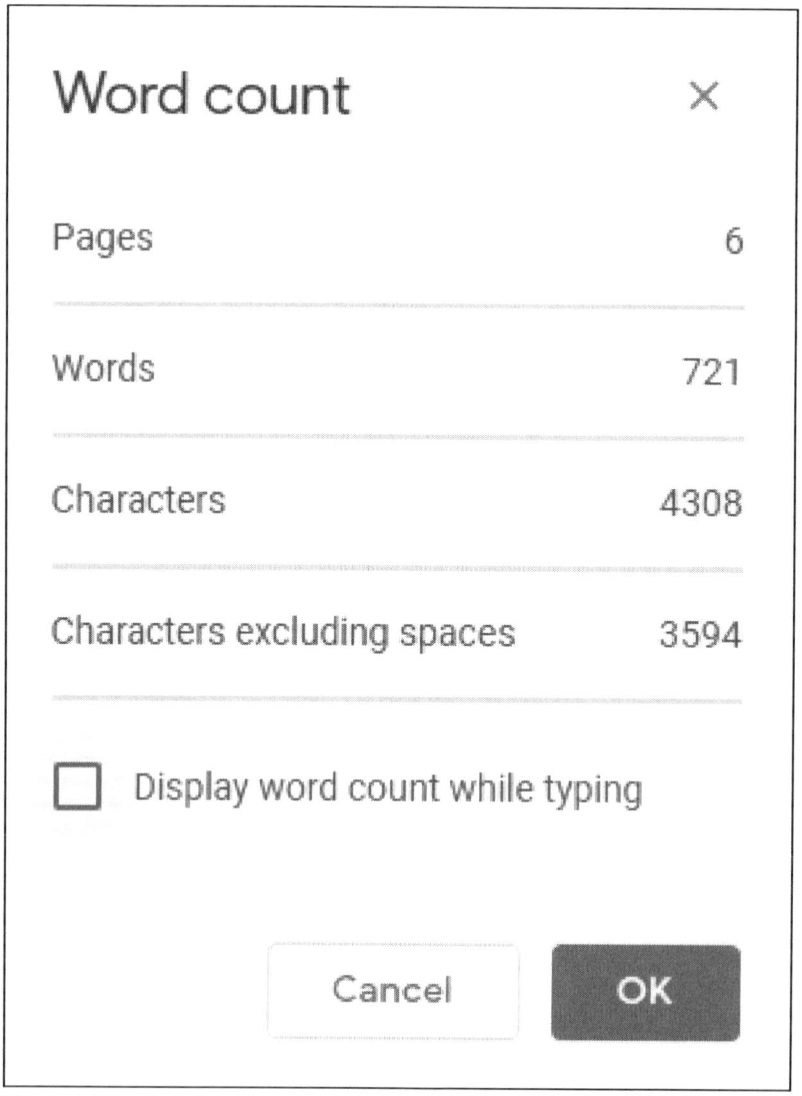

Word count   ✕

Pages	6
Words	721
Characters	4308
Characters excluding spaces	3594

☐ Display word count while typing

Cancel   OK

Figure 4.52

If you check the box that says *Display word count while typing* then that will show you how many words you have in your document in a box that will always be shown in the lower left hand corner of the Docs window.

Figure 4.53

Then if you click the down arrow to see the same information as you saw in figure 4.52.

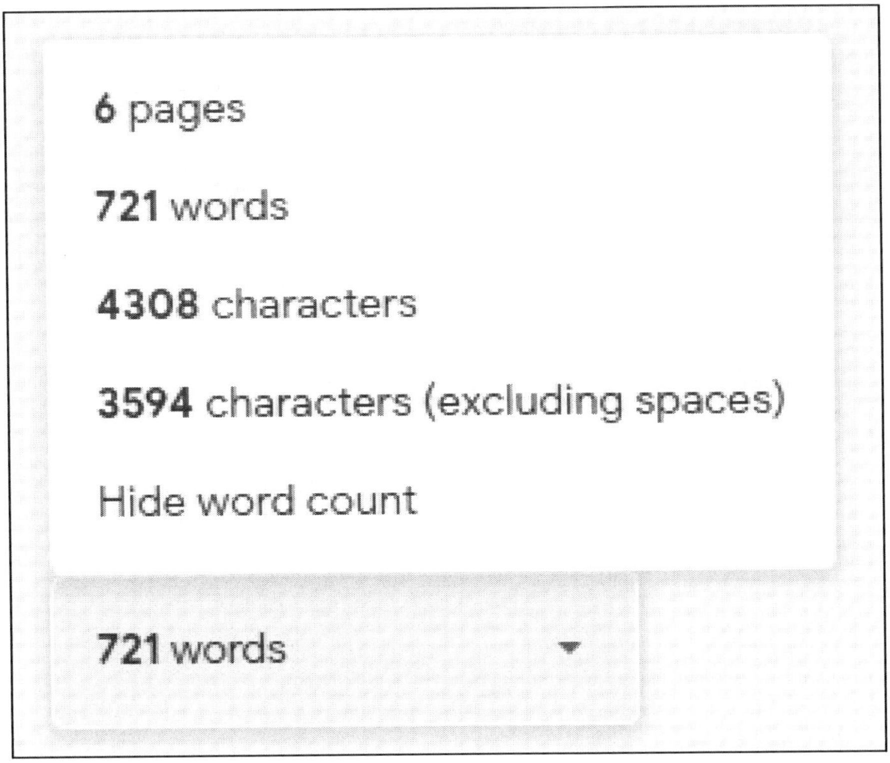

Figure 4.54

Chapter 5 – Sharing and Collaboration

One of the best reasons to use an online word processor is the ability to easily share your work with others and allow them to work on your documents themselves without having to constantly email copies of the document back and forth to each other. When you use the old school email method then you can end up with multiple copies of the same document and it's much harder to keep track of which one is the latest version. Plus every time someone makes a change you will need to wait for them to email the document back to you.

When you share documents online with Docs, you can have multiple people working on the same document and once they make a change, you can see the updates right away and also see who made what changes. You can also do things such as suggest changes or accept or reject edits from other people. And if you are the document owner, you can decide who can edit your documents and who can just view them.

Sharing Documents

Sharing a document is a fairly easy process but there are a few choices you need to make when doing so, otherwise you might not give the person the permission they need to make changes to the document, or you might end up giving someone more access than they need.

To share your document, you can click on the *Share* button at the top right of the page next to your profile picture or letter.

Figure 5.1

Then you will have two options as to how you can share your document. You can have Docs send an invitation to an email address or you can create a link to your document that you can send out yourself.

The top section of figure 5.2 is where you would type in the email address of the person you want Docs to send an invitation to and the bottom section is where you can have Docs create a link that you can email to anyone that you wish to be able to access your document.

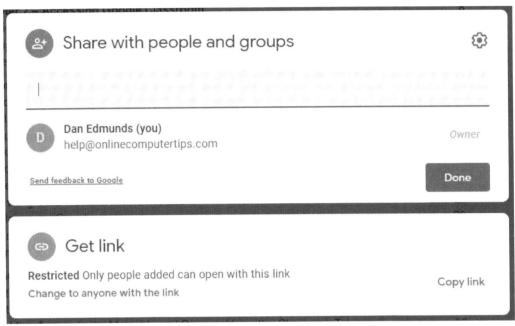

Figure 5.2

You might want to check the settings you have when you click on the gear icon at the top right to make sure that they fit with what you want your fellow collaborators to be able to do with your document.

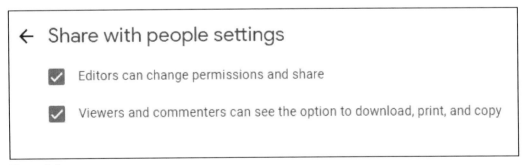

Figure 5.3

If you want to use the link method to share your document then you might want to click on the section where it says *Change to anyone with the link* to make sure that the permissions are set the way you want them to be. You have the option to have the person (or people) who has the link be a viewer, commenter or editor of your document so you need to make sure you don't give them more access than they need.

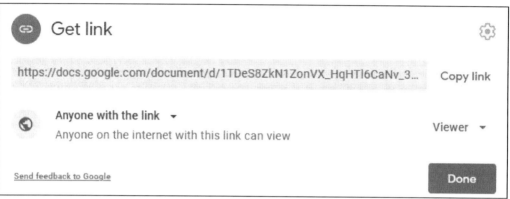

Figure 5.4

After you get the permissions the way you want them simply click on *Copy link* and then you can paste it into an email, chat, or any other method you might use to send it to other people to who you would like to have access to your document.

For my example, I will be using the invitation method to send to a coworker named Todd Simms. So I will type in his email address, add a short message for him, change his permission level to editor and then click on the *Send* button to have the invitation sent to his email address.

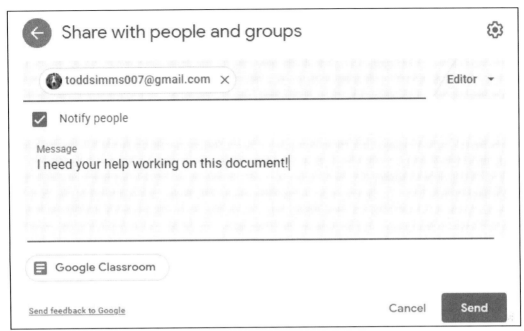

Figure 5.5

Figure 5.6 shows an example of how the email will look when Todd opens it up from his inbox. He can then click on the button that says *Open in Docs* to open my document and he can then start working on it.

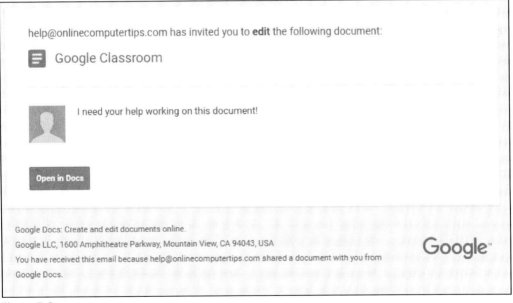

Figure 5.6

If I need to share my document with other people I can simply send out another invitation or copy the link and send it to them that way.

If you will be sharing your document with more than one person using different permission levels, make sure you send separate invitations or links with the appropriate permissions, so you don't accidentally give someone more access than you had planned.

If you share your document with someone and make them an editor then they will be able to share your document with others and also make them editors so be careful when planning out your permission levels. If you share a document with someone and give them view access only, they will still be able to share the document with others (unless you changed this in the settings) but only give them viewer access as well and won't be able to adjust the sharing permissions as seen in figure 5.7.

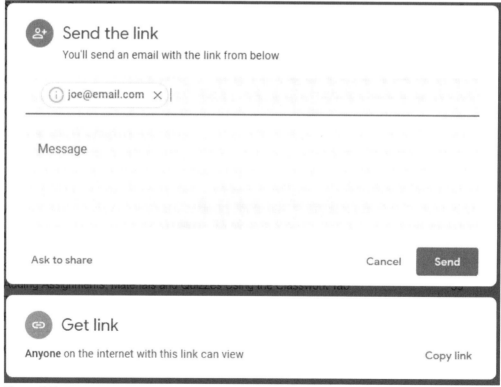

Figure 5.7

If you happen to be working with a document where you only have viewer level access then you can click the button that says *Request edit access* and that will send a message to the document owner. Then if they decide to give you edit access, you will receive a message telling you that you can now edit the document.

Figure 5.8

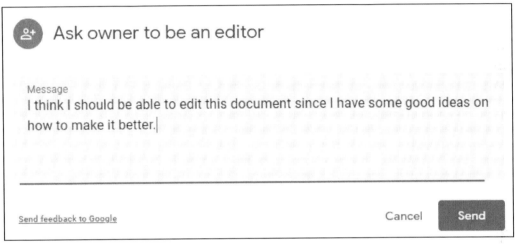

Figure 5.9

One other thing I wanted to mention because you might run into it at some point is that you might see users in your documents with the name *Anonymous* and then some type of animal name after it such as *Anonymous Leopard* as shown in figure 5.10. This happens when you or someone shares a link to your document, and someone is using that link to view your document but was not actually invited by you. Or they might be viewing your document without being logged into their Google account. So if you see this, it doesn't necessarily mean your document has been hacked and there is most likely no reason to panic.

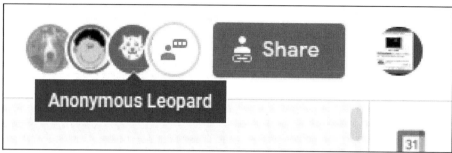

Figure 5.10

Seeing Changes Made By Other Users

If you plan on sharing your documents with other people for the purpose of collaboration then you will most likely want to see what changes they have made to your work. This is where using the version history will help you out. To see the available versions of your documents you can go to the *File* menu and then click on *Version history>See version history*. You can also click on the link in the toolbar which will take you to the latest edit of the file (figure 5.11).

Figure 5.11

When you open the version history you will be shown the most recent version on the top and then other versions below that. The names of the people who have edited the document will be shown under the date they made their changes. You can click on any one of these versions to see what was changed in your document.

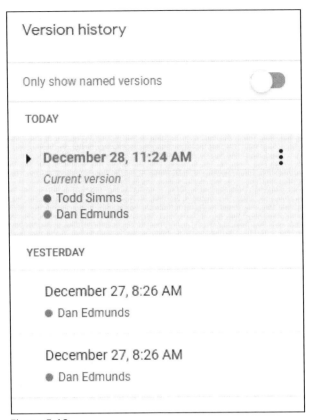

Figure 5.12

When I click on the latest version of my document, Any changes that have been made will be highlighted in different colors that correspond to different users. When I hover my mouse over a particular highlighted area, it will show the name of the person who made that edit. If something has been added, it will just be highlighted but if something has been changed then it will show the original content crossed out and then the new content as highlighted.

When it comes to online learning, it's important to have a system that is easy to use yet can utilize all of the functionality of a real life in person classroom such as assigning tasks to students, having interactive live meetings and testing them on what they have learned. Plus of course you also need a way to grade your students based on their performance. And we all know how important grades are!

Google Classroom has been around for some time now and is always being improved upon to make it easier to use and more capable as an online teaching and learning tool. With Classroom you can host various classes with specific students in each class and also have the same students in multiple many different classes. You can also prepare lesson plans, assignments, quizzes and other material specific to each one of your classes or share the content between some or all of your classes.

Figure 5.13

If you want to name a particular version of an edit you can click on the three vertical dots next to that date and then choose *Name this version* to give it a more descriptive name.

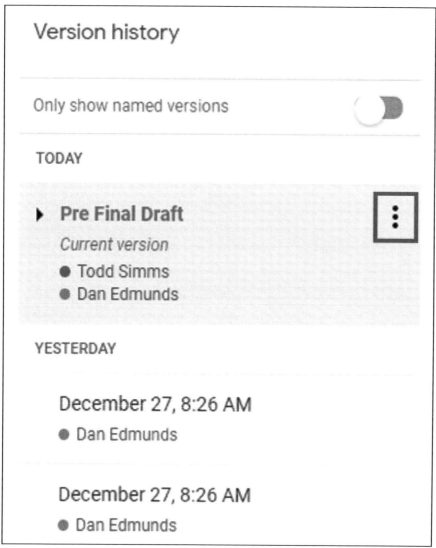

Figure 5.14

You can also do this from the *File* menu and *Version history>Name current version* option while you have that particular version of the file open.

If you have an older version that you would like to make the current version then you can go to the three vertical dots next to that version and choose *Restore this version* which will make that version the current version after you click on the *Restore* button.

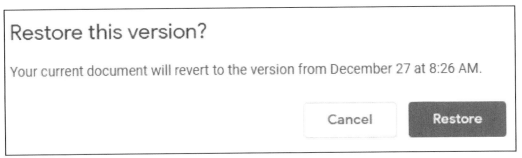

Figure 5.15

Then when you go back to your version history you will see it at the top of the list with a note saying it's now the current version and the date it was restored from.

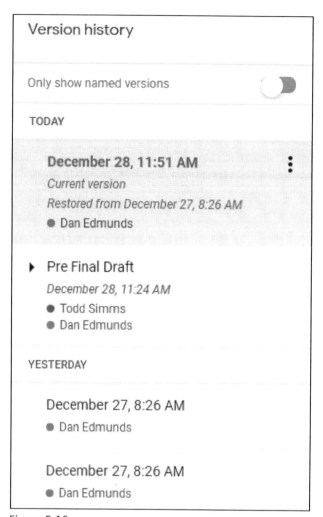

Figure 5.16

Another thing you can do to see what your fellow collaborators are working on is to click on their icon to the left of the Share button. When you do this, it will take you to the place in the document that they are currently working so you can see exactly what they are working on.

Figure 5.17

Chatting With Collaborators

Once you start working with shared documents you will notice that you will see other users next to your user icon at the top right of the page. This happens when these other users also have your document open in their Google Docs app. Figure 5.18 shows that there are two other users that have this document open along with my user.

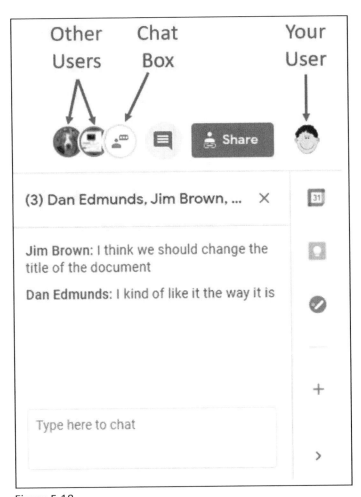

Figure 5.18

The chat box is used to send messages to the other users who currently have your document open in real time. This way you can discuss your work without having to get on a conference call or Zoom meeting etc. Once you click on the chat box icon you will be able to send messages to everyone that currently has your document open.

 If you would like to improve your Zoom video conferencing skills then check out my book titled **Zoom Made Easy**.
https://www.amazon.com/dp/B088B96YNK

This chat box will also show you when someone closes the document and also when someone reopens or opens the document.

(3) Dan Edmunds, Jim Brown, ...   X

Jim Brown: I think we should change the title of the document

Dan Edmunds: I kind of like it the way it is

Todd Simms has left.
Dan Edmunds has left.
Todd Simms has opened the document.

Figure 5.19

Editing, Suggesting and Viewing Modes
Now that you know how to share your documents and assign permissions to your users, I would like to go over the various modes that you and your collaborators can use while working on a document. The current mode of your document can be found under the Share button.

I mentioned before that the default mode that you will be in when working on your own documents is Editing mode. This mode allows you to make changes to your documents as well as rename them, print them, delete them, share them and so on.

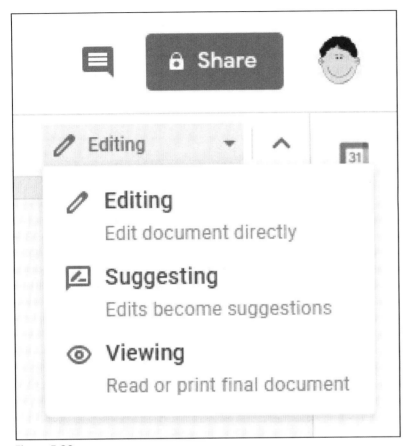

Figure 5.20

If you only have viewer access to a document then you won't even see these options under your Share button since you can't change your permission level. Speaking of the Viewer level, this only allows you to view and print a document and you won't be able to make any changes and can only give the viewer permission to others if you share the document yourself.

Suggesting mode is a little more complicated but what it will do is allow you to make suggested changes without actually changing the document content (figure 5.21). When you are in suggesting mode, any changes you made will be highlighted in green and if you replace or remove some text or an image etc., it will still be shown there but it will have a line through it. Then when the owner opens the document they will see the changes you have made and then be able to either accept your changes or deny them (figure 5.22). They will also get notified of these suggestions so they will know that they need to take a look at them.

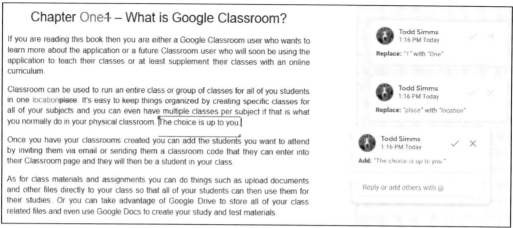

Figure 5.21

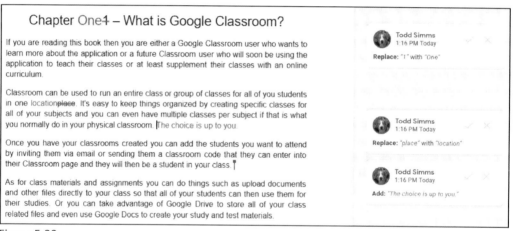

Figure 5.22

To accept a suggestion, simply click on the checkmark next to that suggestion and to reject it, click on the X. Suggesting mode is a great way to add your own input to a document without actually changing it and risk getting someone upset with you in case they don't like your changes.

Commenting

Commenting works in a similar fashion to making suggestions but rather than making the actual changes you are just making comments about a particular area of the document.

To make a comment, simply highlight the area you want to comment on and then click the Add comment button on the right side of the page. You can also click the *Add comment* button in the toolbar.

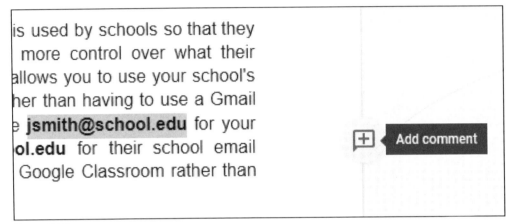

Figure 5.23

Next you can type in your comment in the box and then click the Comment button when you are finished.

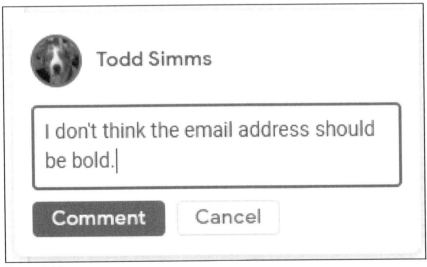

Figure 5.24

Now when someone else who has editor rights goes into that document they will be able to see the comments and can click on the checkmark to mark it as resolved or they can click on the three vertical dots to create a link to that comment. Then when they send someone that link, they will be able to go directly to that comment within the document rather than have to search for it.

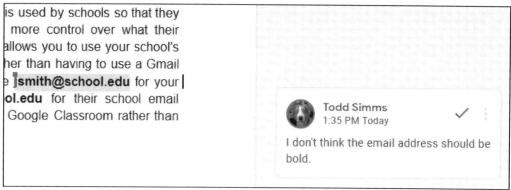

Figure 5.25

When you comment on something in a document, the owner of that document will also get an email showing your comment and can act on it from there.

As the document owner, you can assign tasks to specific people by entering their name or email address after the @ (or +) symbol. Docs should bring up a list of people with who you have shared the document with after you type @ so you can just pick from the list rather than needing to know the person's email address.

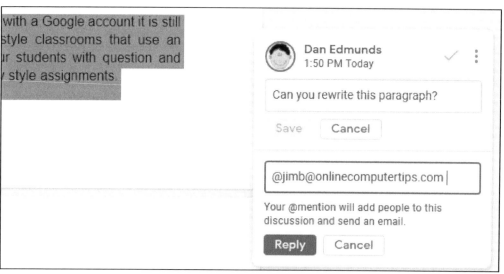

Figure 5.26

Then that person will receive an email with your comment as well as the text you highlighted for that particular comment.

Dan Edmunds mentioned you in a comment in the following document

Google Classroom

Even though Google Classroom can be used by anyone with a Google account it is still geared more towards traditional teachers with typical style classrooms that use an assignment and grading type system. You can test your students with question and answer style quizzes, multiple choice tests and also essay style assignments.

Dan Edmunds

Can you rewrite this paragraph?

Dan Edmunds **New**

@jimb@onlinecomputertips.com

Open

Figure 5.27

Also when that person opens the document containing the comment and goes to that section of the document they will see the highlighted text as well as the comment itself. They can then click the checkmark to mark it as resolved if they are finished with their requested updates.

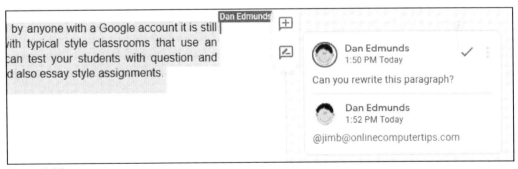

Figure 5.28

If you would like to see all of the comments that have been made on a particular document then you can click the *Open comment history* button to see who made what comments (figure 5.29).

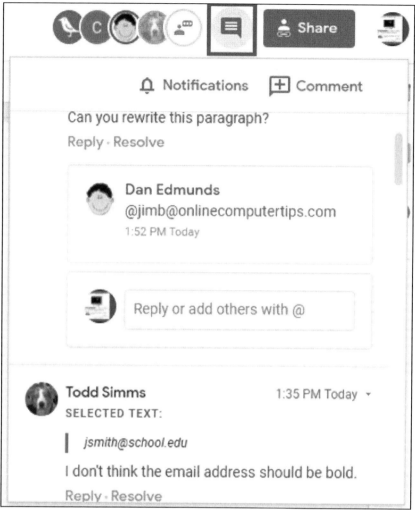

Figure 5.29

Emailing Collaborators

If you need to send certain people a message about something you need them to review or change with your document then you can email your collaborators rather than post comments that everyone will be able to see. Keep in mind that this is different than emailing a copy of your document to someone which is also something you can do and something I will be discussing later in this chapter.

When you go to the *File* menu and then *Email>Email collaborators*, Docs will automatically include all the people that have access to your document, and you can then decide who you want to send your message to. If there is someone in the list who should not receive the message then you can click the X by their email address. You can also choose to send the message to all the document viewers, document editors or both with the appropriate checkboxes (figure 5.30).

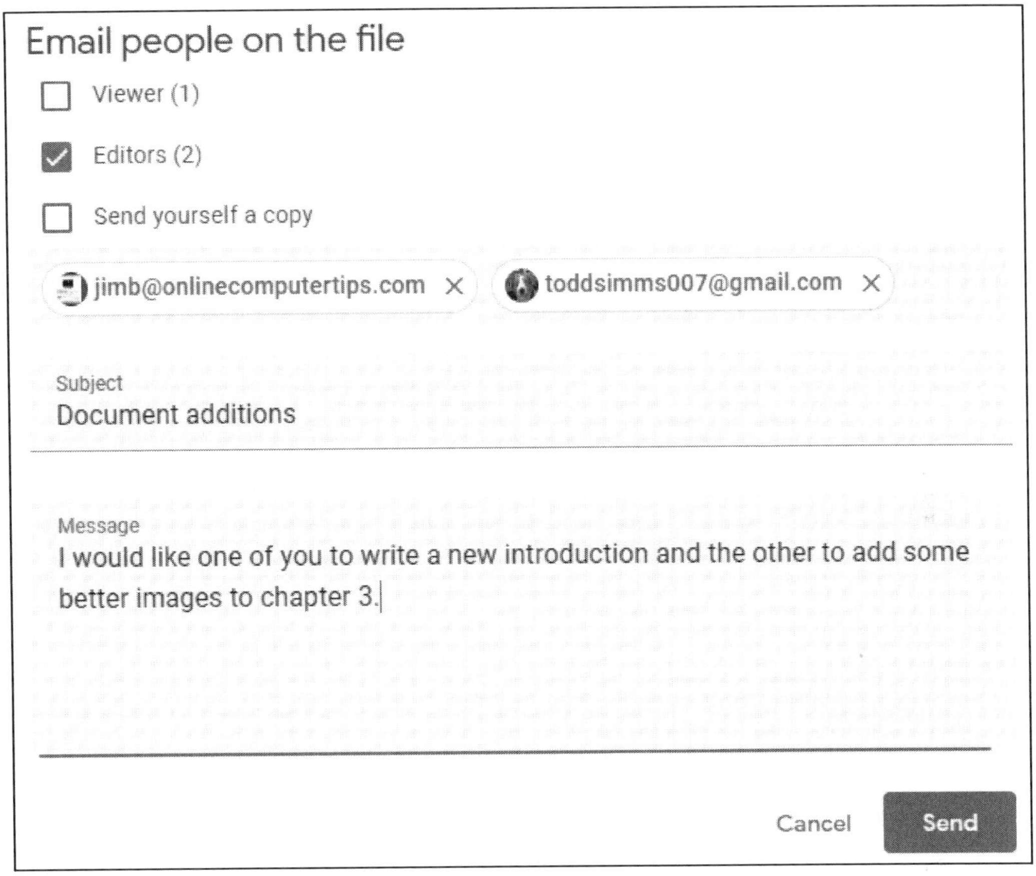

Email people on the file

☐ Viewer (1)

☑ Editors (2)

☐ Send yourself a copy

jimb@onlinecomputertips.com ✕   toddsimms007@gmail.com ✕

Subject
Document additions

Message
I would like one of you to write a new introduction and the other to add some better images to chapter 3.

Cancel   **Send**

Figure 5.30

Then everyone who you sent the email to will get the same copy of the message in their inbox with a clickable link to the document.

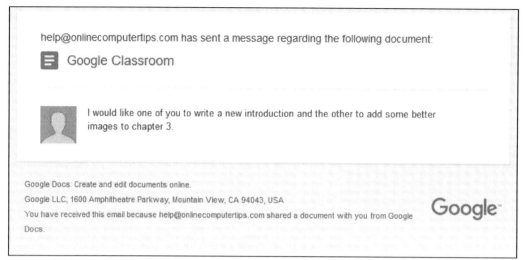

Figure 5.31

Downloading Your Documents and Making Copies

Just because Google Docs is a cloud based application doesn't mean you have to work on your files exclusively via your web browser. Docs offers the ability to download your documents in a variety of formats so you can work on them in different programs or without needing to have an internet connection to access your documents online.

To download your document you can go to the *File* menu and then choose *Download*. From there you will be presented with several file types that you can save your document as. For example, you can save your document as a Microsoft Word document or a PDF document since these are commonly used file types.

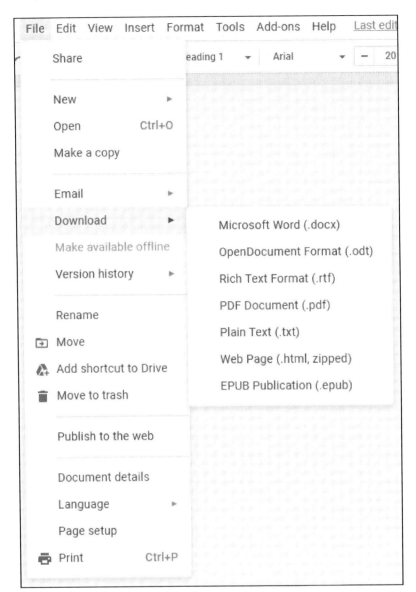

Figure 5.32

Once you choose your file type, Docs will convert the file for you and then allow you to download it right to the hard drive on your computer. Then you can open it up and work on it within the corresponding application. Just keep in mind that when if you want to sync your changes back to "the cloud", you will need to upload your file to your Google Drive, and it will stay in the same format in which you download it as. You can still open many file types within Docs so if you have a Word Document uploaded to your Drive, you can easily open it with Docs.

You can also go to your Google Drive, find your document and then download it to your computer since Docs will convert the file to Word format before you actually download it.

 If you would like to learn more about online file storage and backup solutions then check out my book titled **Cloud Storage Made Easy**.
https://www.amazon.com/dp/1730838359

Now let's say you have a lot of people that will be working on your document and you would like to save a copy of it elsewhere before they start making changes. What you can do in this case is make a copy of your document so then you will have your own copy that you can keep in its original state or make your own edits without having others make any changes.

To make a copy of a document simply open that document, go to the *File* menu and then choose *Make a copy* and you can then give your copied document a new name and decide where you want to save it. The default location is within your Drive but you can click on *My Drive* and choose a different folder within your drive or save it to your computer if you like.

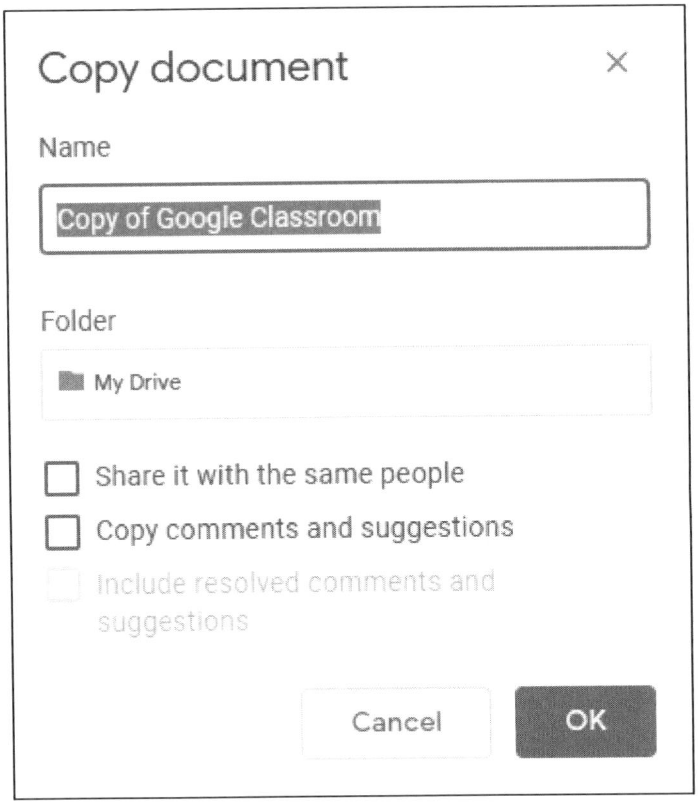

Figure 5.33

You will also have the option to share the copied document with the same people you shared the original with and you can also have any comments or suggestions (including resolved suggestions) copied over to your copied document as well.

Once you click the *OK* button, Docs will open up the copied version of your document and you can then start working on it if you desire.

Emailing Documents

If you are working with other people and don't know if they have a Google account or know if they have even used Docs before then you can email them a copy of your document right from Docs. That way they will have their own copy to do with as they please.

When you email someone a copy of your document, any changes they make to it will only be saved on that copy and your original online copy will not be updated. In other words, they will not be shared collaborator with your team if they are using the emailed copy of the document.

To email a copy of your document go to the *File* menu and then choose *Email>Email this file*. Then you can enter the email address or addresses of the people you wish to send a copy of your file to. You can also include a message in the email if you like. The box that says *Don't attach. Include content in the email* will have the contents of the document be displayed in the body of the email rather than sending an actual Docs file. This option won't be the best way to go for most people.

Figure 5.34

Underneath that, you have a dropdown selection for what type of file you would like the email attachment to be sent as. If you don't want anyone to edit your file then I would choose PDF even though it won't completely secure your document from being edited but it's better than the other options.

Once you click on *Send*, Docs will convert your document and send it to everyone you had listed as a recipient. When the people you sent the copy to get their email it will arrive as an attached file in whatever format you chose. Figure 5.35 shows my email that has a PDF copy of my file attached.

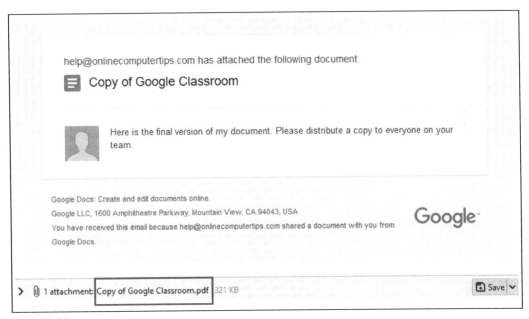

Figure 5.35

Create Links to Other Documents From Your Google Drive

Even though the next chapter in this book will be on Google Drive, I wanted to show you a couple of ways you can share your files from your Drive itself. Once you are in your drive you will have the option to share or create a link to your files so you can then share them with others.

Once you are in your Drive, find the file you wish to share and then right click on it. You will have many options to choose from, but I will be focusing on the *Share* and *Get link* options as seen in figure 5.36

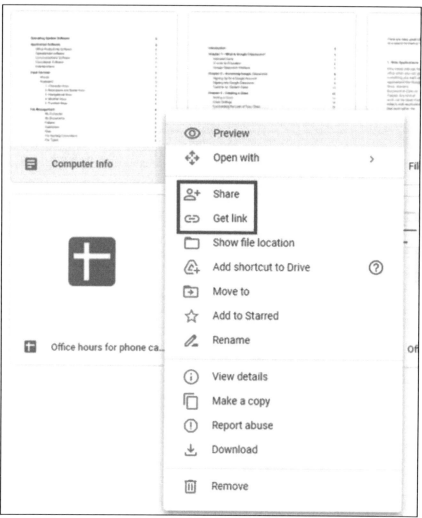

Figure 5.36

The *Share* option will bring up the *Share with people and groups* dialog box that we were just working with earlier in this chapter and works exactly the same way.

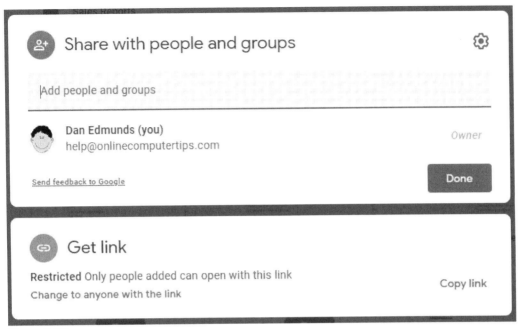

Figure 5.37

The *Get link* option will bring up the familiar create a shared link dialog box with the link already created. You can then choose the permission level you want to be assigned to the link and copy the link to paste it into an email etc.

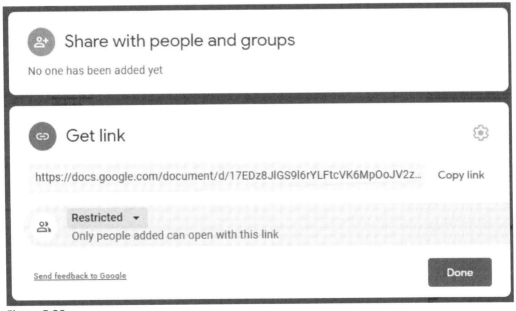

Figure 5.38

Publishing to the Web

Another way to share a document is to publish or post it on a website that can be accessed with a URL (website address). Normally when you host content on a website you need to be able to create web pages and then have a place where you upload your content to then be hosted, usually for a fee.

With Docs, you can have Google post your content on a web page that they provide for free and then all you need to do is copy the link\address for this page and paste it into an email etc. to share it with others.

The main thing you need to be aware of here is when you use the publish to the web option, nobody else will be able to edit or comment on your file etc. since it will be a view only copy, just like content on other web pages.

To start the publishing process you will go to the *File* menu and then choose *Publish to the web*. Next you will need to decide if you are going to have Docs create a link or embedded code that you can add to an existing website. If you do not have an existing website that you want to add your document to then you will choose the *Link* option.

In the Published content & settings area you can choose whether or not Docs will republish your content when you make changes to your document. So if you want to keep your document and webpage in sync, you will check the box that says *Automatically republish when changes are made*. Once you are ready to go click on *Start publishing* and you will be prompted to confirm that you want your document to be live on a web page.

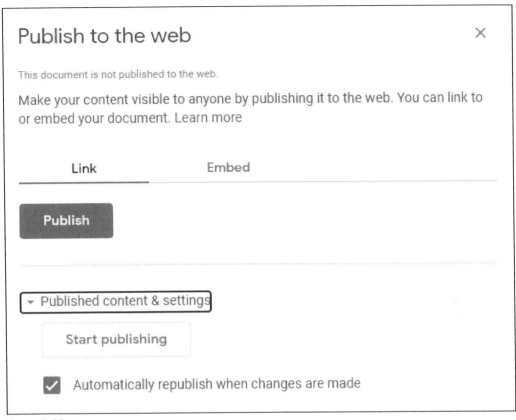

Figure 5.39

Figure 5.40

Then you will be given a link to the published content that you can copy and paste wherever you need it. It's a good idea to paste the link into the address bar of your web browser to make sure your content looks the way you want it to on the web page.

When you are done sharing your content online, you can click on the *Stop publishing* button to have your document removed from the web page.

Figure 5.41

Chapter 6 - Google Drive

Since I have been talking about Google Drive throughout this book I thought it would be a good idea to devote a chapter to the topic since you will most likely be using Google Drive quite a bit if you plan on being a serious Google Docs user. Since I went over sharing files from Drive in the last chapter, I will not be discussing it again here.

Introducing Google Drive
Since many of the Google Apps in addition to Docs rely on storing documents in the cloud, you really should have a solid understanding of how Google Drive works since this is the place you will most likely be using to store the files that you use with many of your other Google Apps.

Everyone has heard of Google, and they seem to be getting their hands more and more into other areas of technology, so it only seems appropriate that they would be involved in the cloud storage business. (And they have been involved in the cloud storage business for some time now.)

The cloud storage service provided by Google used to be just called Google Drive, but recently they have changed the name to rebrand their cloud storage solution to Google One. Now they offer family plans and even things like special hotel pricing as a way to entice you into signing up. In other words, the new Google One name includes more than just online storage, but you can also combine things like Google Photos and Gmail to simplify your Google services. Even though the new name is Google One, they still call the storage portion of the plan Google Drive, so that is what I will be focusing on for this chapter.

The Google Drive Interface
If you haven't already figured out how to get into your Google Drive app then it's pretty simple to do. If you open your web browser and go to the Google home page you can get to it from the Google waffle icon like you did to open Google Docs (figure 6.1). And don't forget that you can drag the Drive icon closer to the top if it's something you plan on using all the time. You can also access Google Drive from https://drive.google.com/ and if you are logged into your Google account it will take you right to your files and folders.

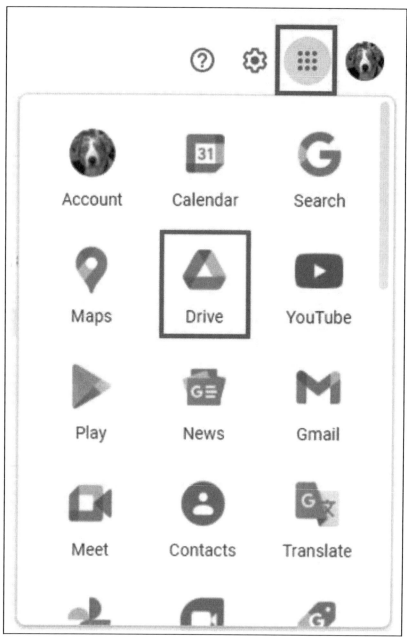

Figure 6.1

Once you open Drive you will see any files and folders that you have created as shown in figure 6.2. If you are new to Drive then you most likely won't have any folders and might not even have any files yet. I will be going over how to create folders and upload files in the next section.

Figure 6.2

At the top of the Drive interface is a search box where you can search for documents using a word or phrase. You can even search by email address to find documents that were created or shared by a particular person.

If you don't like the thumbnail view for your files then you can click on the view options button to change it to more of a list\details view as seen in figure 6.3. Then you can click on the column name to sort by name, owner, modified date or file size.

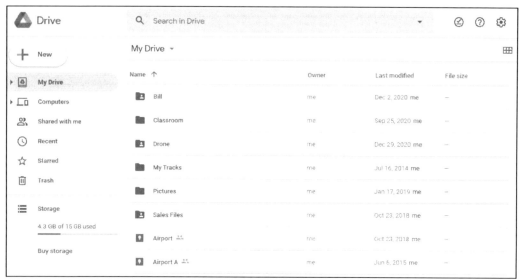

Figure 6.3

The navigation area has several components and here is what each one of them does.

- **New** – If you want to create a new folder or upload a file from your computer then you can do so from here (figure 6.4). I will show you a couple of ways to do this in the next section. You can also start a new Google Docs, Sheets, Slides, or Form file from here and it will be saved right to your Drive. There are some other apps that you can open from the *More* menu choice as well.

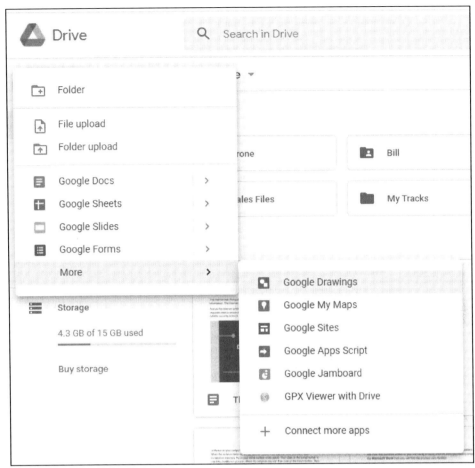

Figure 6.4

- **My Drive** – The My Drive section is the default view which we saw in figure 6.2. If you click on the down arrow next to My Drive then you will be shown your folder list underneath the My Drive icon and you can access any one of them from here.

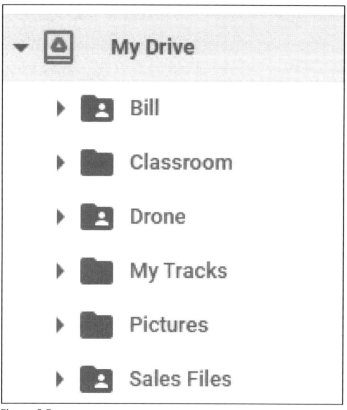

Figure 6.5

- **Computers** – If you use the Drive desktop client to sync your files between your computer and your Drive account then your computer will be shown here. If you have never used the desktop client then you won't have this choice shown. I will be going over the Drive client later in this chapter.

- **Shared with me** – This section gives you a quick way to access files that have been shared with you by other people.

- **Recent** – Here you will find files that you have recently worked on. So rather than have to go find where you have them saved you can just open them from here. Think of this as a shortcut to your recently used files.

- **Starred** – If you have files that you use all the time or that you want to be reminded of then you can star them so they will show up here. Think of starred files as favorites\bookmarks that you use in your web browser. To add a file to your starred section simply select that file in Drive and go to the three vertical dots at the top right of the window and choose *Add to Starred*.

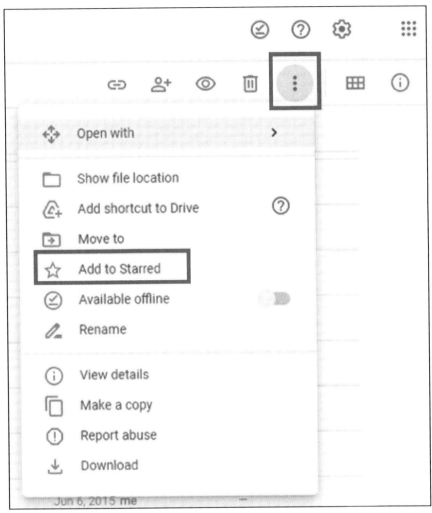

Figure 6.6

- **Trash** – When you delete a file, it will go to your Trash similar to how files go to the Recycle Bin in Windows when you delete them. You can recover files from the trash if needed by right clicking on them and choosing *Restore*.

Google is always changing how they do things with their apps and just about everything else including how long you can keep items in the trash. You used to be able to keep them forever but now they say they will automatically empty files from your trash after 30 days so keep that in mind. As of now I have items older than 30 days in my trash but that might soon change!

- **Storage** – Here is where you can see how much of your free online storage you are using as well as what files are taking up what amount of space. Google will give you 15GB of space for free but if you need more then you will need to sign up for one of their subscription plans or just make another Google account.

Creating Folders and Uploading Files

As you should know by now, when you create a new Google Doc, it is automatically saved in your Drive and now you should know that you can go to the *New* button and create a new document from there that will also be saved in your drive.

If you plan on keeping your files organized then you should consider creating folders to help you do this. Once you create a folder you can then save new documents into that folder or move existing documents into that folder (and other files).

To create a new folder, click on the *New* button (or right click in a blank area) and choose *Folder*. Then give your folder a name and click on *Create*. You will then have your new folder shown with your other folders ready to be used.

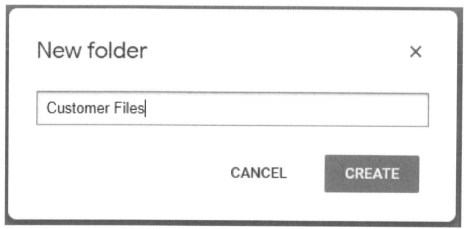

Figure 6.7

To upload a file or folder from your computer click on *New* and can then choose the *File Upload* or *Folder Upload* option and then browse to that file or folder on your local computer and choose *Open* (for files) or *Upload* (for folders).

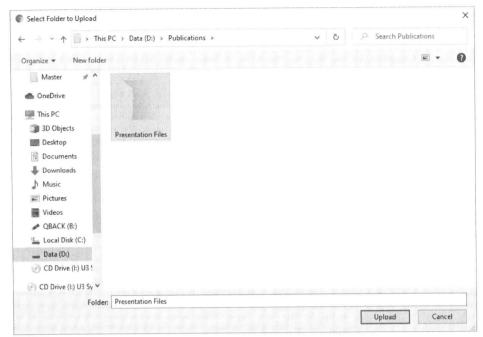

Figure 6.8

Another way to upload files and folders into Drive is to use the drag and drop method like you would use when working with the files and folders on your desktop computer. All you need to do is have your Drive open on one part of your screen and your file or folder location open in another window on your screen and drag and drop your files or folders right into your browser.

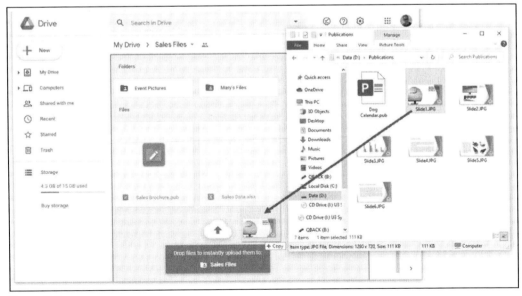

Figure 6.9

Managing Files and Folders

If you end up using Drive to store a lot of files and folders then you will need to know how to manage these files and folders, so things don't get lost and it doesn't take you 20 minutes just to find a file that you need to access.

One of the easiest ways to manage your files and folders is to right click on the one you want to work with and choose the appropriate option from there. Figure 6.10 shows the choices you have when right clicking on each type and as you can see, the options are fairly similar.

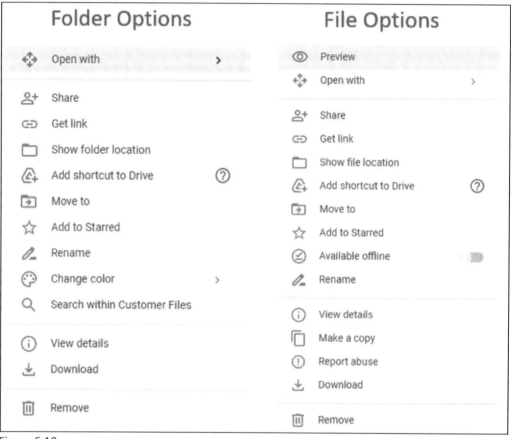

Figure 6.10

I will now go over some of the choices that I feel you should know about since you will probably be using these options more than the others.

- **Share and Get link** – I went over how to share your files from Drive in Chapter 5, but you can get to these share settings by right clicking on a file or folder as well.

- **Move to** – If you need to move a file or folder into a different folder then you can use this option to simply select the folder you wish to move the item into.

- **Rename** – Use this option to rename any files or folders and they will be instantly updated. It should also be updated for anyone who you share the file or folder with.

- **View details** – If you would like to see information about a certain file or folder, you can use this option to see things such as the created date, when the item was last modified and who it is shared with (figure 6.11). The *Activity* tab will show details about things such as when you changed the file or when you shared it etc.

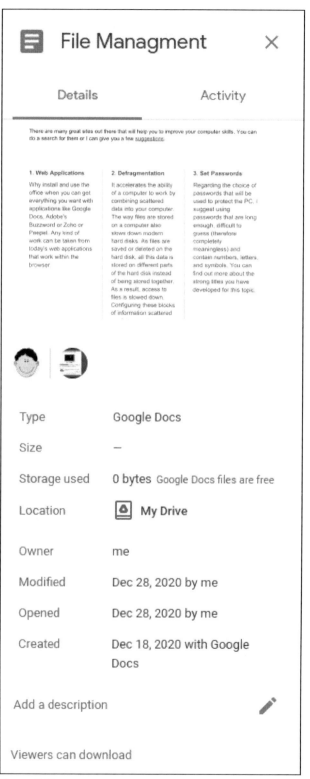

Figure 6.11

 If you take a look at figure 6.11 where it says *Storage used*, you will notice that is shows *0 bytes*. This is because files such as Google Docs and Sheets don't count against your total Drive storage space. The area that says *Type* will let you know if your file is a Google Doc file or if it's another type such as a Microsoft Word file.

- **Download** – If you would like to have a copy of a file or folder stored on your local computer then you can download it to your PC using this option.

- **Remove** – This option will send the file or folder to your Trash where it can be restored later if needed.

Google Drive Desktop Client (Backup and Sync)

If you are the type who is used to working with your files and folders on your local PC rather than online then you can use the Google Drive desktop client and have the best of both worlds. The desktop client was designed to let you access your Drive files and folders from your computer like you would any other type of file or folder yet keep them synchronized with the files and folders in your Drive online. You can also use the Drive client to synchronize\backup other files that you have on your computer that are not kept in your Drive.

If you take a look at figure 6.12 you can see that the Computers section is missing under My Drive on the left side of the screen. This is because this user has not installed the desktop client on their computer and logged in with their account.

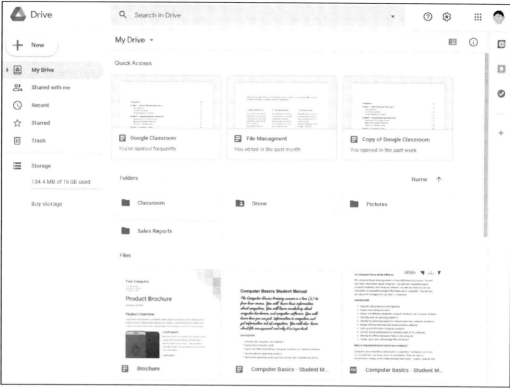

Figure 6.12

Now if I go to the gear icon at the top right of the page I can click on *Get Drive for desktop* to be taken to the client download page.

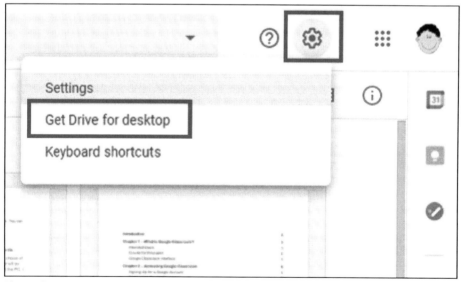

Figure 6.13

Once I am at the download page I will want to find the section for individuals and look for the download link. Depending on when Google decides to change the way this page is designed, it might look a little different for you.

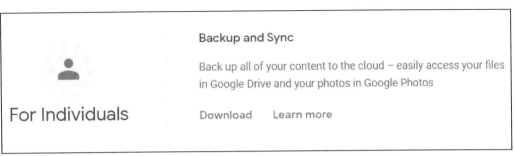

Figure 6.14

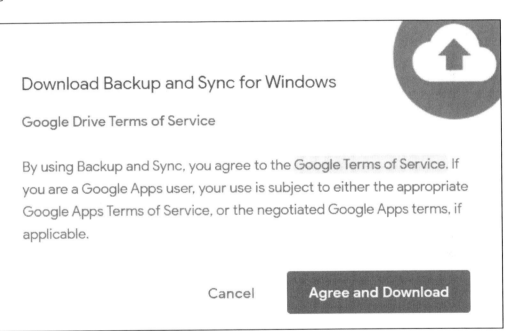

Figure 6.15

The installation process for the Drive client should be automatic and once it's done you will need to log in with your Google account to get started and go through a verification process that usually involves sending a notification to your phone that you need to acknowledge.

Once you are verified you will be asked which folders from your computer you want to have synced\backed up to your Drive.

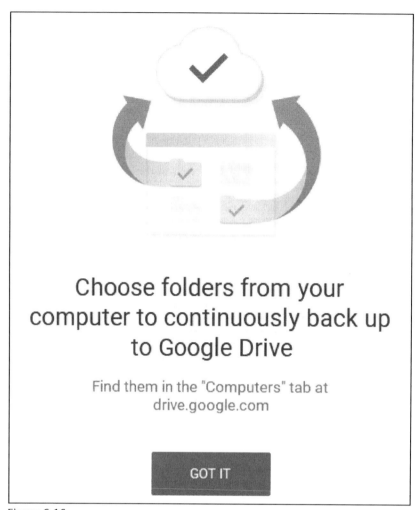

Figure 6.16

By default it will want to backup everything on your desktop, in your documents folder and also your pictures folder. You can check or uncheck the boxes next to these items to configure it however you like. For my example, I just want to backup a certain folder on my computer so I will uncheck all 3 of those boxes and click on the *Choose Folder* link to find my specific folder.

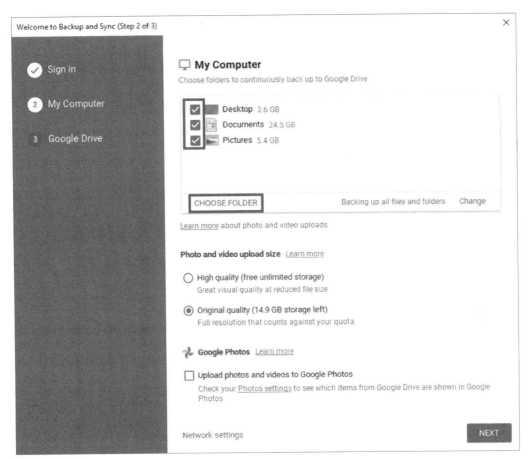

Figure 6.17

Now that I have browsed to my *Client Files* folder and unchecked the other three folders my selection looks like figure 6.18.

Figure 6.18

185

Later when I go back to my Drive in my browser I will see that I have the *Computers* section with my Client Files folder shown.

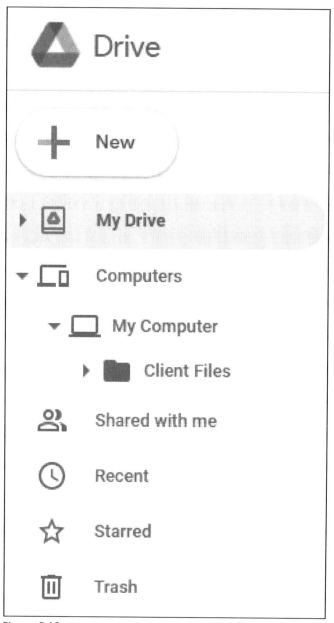

Figure 6.19

You will also be prompted to sync your Drive files and folders with your PC during the Drive client configuration process.

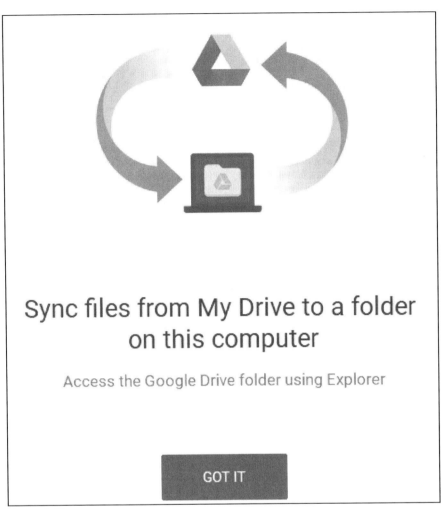

Figure 6.20

You can choose to have all the files and folders from your online Drive be synced to your computer or choose which ones you would like to have synchronized by clicking on *Sync only these folders* and then check the ones you want to use.

The *Folder location* section is where the Drive client will copy and sync your Drive files on your local computer. By default it will go to your Users folder under your profile name, but you can change that by clicking on the *Change* link.

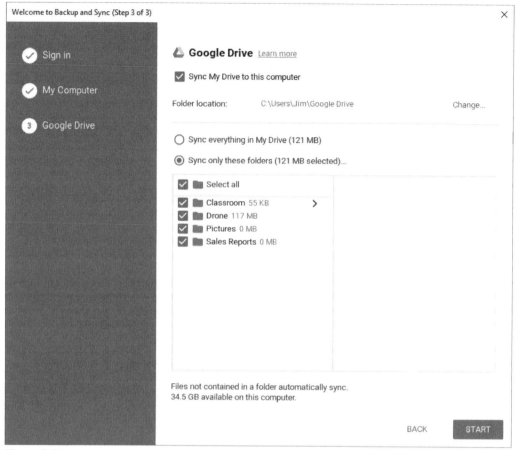

Figure 6.21

If I go to the Drive folder on my local PC located at *C:\Users\Jim\Google Drive* then I will see that now have the same files that were online stored on my local computer.

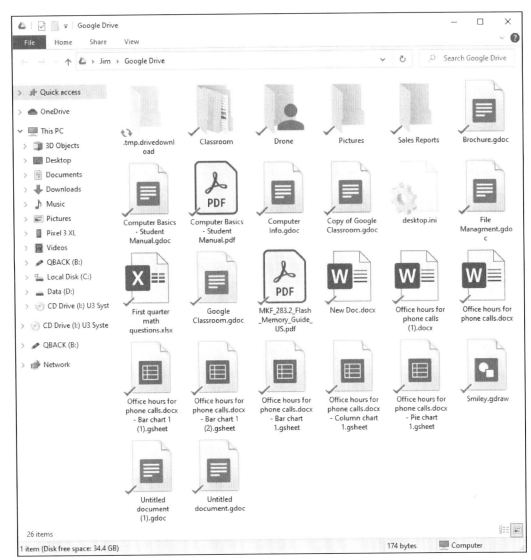

Figure 6.22

Getting used to the Drive client will take a little time since it can be confusing as to what is getting synchronized where so just play around with it a bit and if you don't like what it is doing then you can go to the preferences and modify how your files and folders are being copied. If you are a Windows user then you will find the Drive client in your programs under *Backup and Sync from Google*. You can also find it running in the notification area of your Windows taskbar by the clock.

Chapter 7 – Extra Features

By now you should have a fairly good idea how to use Docs as well as format your documents after you create them. Compared to other programs such as Microsoft Word, Docs is pretty simple and doesn't have too many complex features that you need to worry about learning how to use.

However, there are some additional things you can do with Docs that I haven't gone over that you might find useful. I decided to dedicate a chapter to these features rather than try and spread them out throughout the book so hopefully you will want to try some of them out for yourself!

Document Revision History
I touched on revision history a bit in Chapter 5 but now I would like to go into a little more detail about what it is and how to use it.

Since there is no save option in Docs, it will automatically save your work every time you make a change. So as you can imagine, you can end up with a lot of revisions in a short amount of time.

To see all of your document revisions you can click on the *File* menu and then on *Version history>See version history*. As you can see in figure 7.1 I have some revisions starting on December 27th and going until December 30th and the document was created on December 27th. You can also see over to the left that there have been 9 edits made to this document so far.

I mentioned named versions earlier in the book but once again these are revisions that have been named by you or one of your collaborators. There is a named revision called *Pre Final Draft* that was created on December 28th. The named revisions can help you keep track of what versions contain what updates. You can add up to 40 named versions per document. You can also turn on the slider at the top that says *Only show named versions* if those particular versions are the only ones you care about.

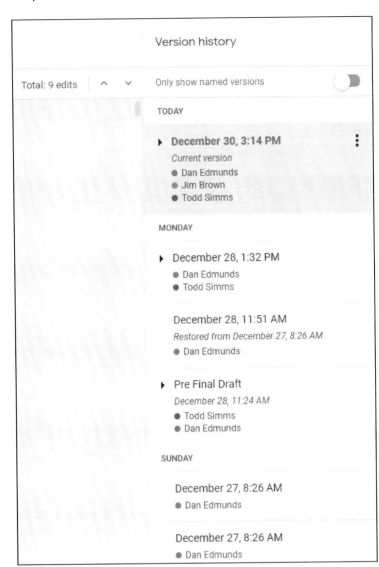

Figure 7.1

For the version of the file from December 30th you can see that there were three people who had worked on the file and made changes. You will also notice that it is the current version but when someone makes changes again it will go down on the list and then there will be a new current version.

As you scroll down your document, you will see the changes that each person made highlighted in the color that matches their name in the version history list. Figure 7.2 shows that a sentence was added to the end of the paragraph by Jim Brown since it's highlighted in his color and when I hover over the sentence with my mouse his name appears.

One great feature of Classroom is the ability to have multiple teachers participate in one class or even have the parents of your students get involved by allowing them to receive information about a student's courses and work once they are invited by the teacher. This way they can keep an eye on their children and see what they are working on and how they are doing. And we all know how we need to keep an eye on our kids!

Figure 7.2

If I were to click on the next version in the list then it would open up that version of the document and only show the changes made by the two people who were editing this particular version (Dan and Todd).

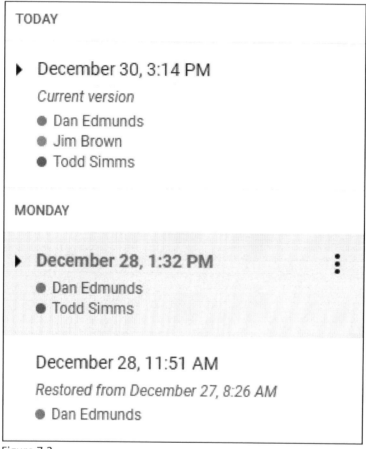

Figure 7.3

The next version on the list says it was restored from December 27th at 8:26 AM and this was a version that I had chosen to restore to make it the current version at that time. But now that there were additional changes, it's not the most current version anymore.

Clicking on the three vertical dots next to the version will give you different options depending on the status of the version you are clicking on.

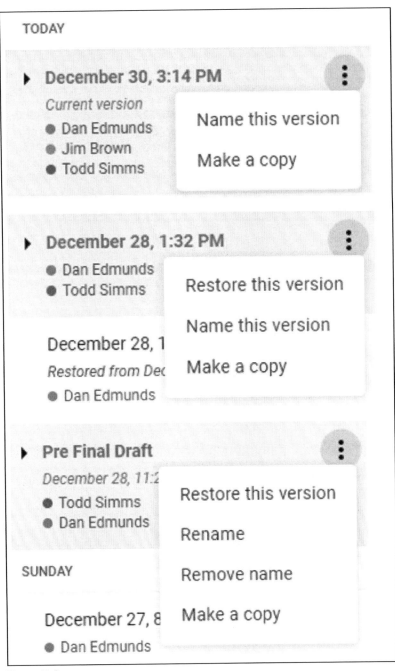

Figure 7.4

Translating a Document Into Another Language

One really cool feature of Docs is the ability to take any of your documents and translate them into another language with just a few clicks of the mouse. So if you need to send your document to someone who doesn't speak your language you can easily convert it to their language and send it off to them. When you do this, Docs will make a copy of your document in the other language, so you don't need to worry about it converting your original document.

Figure 7.5 shows a page of my document in its original language (English) and now I will do the translation by going to the *Tools* menu and then choosing *Translate document*.

Introduction

In today's changing environment we need to be able to adapt and change along with it in order to still be able to get the things done that we need to. This applies to both our work, home and learning environments and if we need to spend all of our time figuring out how to do our work then we will never get any of it done.

When it comes to online learning, it's important to have a system that is easy to use yet can utilize all of the functionality of a real life in person classroom such as assigning tasks to students, having interactive live meetings and testing them on what they have learned. Plus of course you also need a way to grade your students based on their performance.

Google Classroom has been around for some time now and is always being improved upon to make it easier to use and more capable as an online teaching and learning tool. With Classroom you can host various classes with specific students in each class and also have the same students in multiple classes. You can also prepare lesson plans, assignments, quizzes and other material specific to each one of your classes or share the content between some or all of your classes.

The goal of this book is to get you up and running with Google Classroom and show you how to create your classes, add students, distribute your learning materials and grade your student's performance. I will also show you how to join and participate in a class from a student's point of view so you can see how each side works. You will see that there are several ways to accomplish many of the typical tasks you will be performing so you will be able to find the way that works the best for you, or use several methods!

The way you use Google Classroom will most likely vary from the way other teachers or students use it so it is a good idea to know the ins and outs of how it works so you can get your work done no matter where you are within the application. Once you get the hang of Classroom you will find that it's not nearly as difficult as it might appear at the beginning. So on that note, let's start the learning process!

Figure 7.5

Next, I will need to choose the language I will be translating my document into and also a name for the copy of the document that will be created. When I am ready to go I will click on the *Translate* button.

Figure 7.6

Figure 7.7 shows the same page of my original document now translated into my new language (Spanish) and now I can send it off to my Spanish speaking collaborator.

Introducción

En el entorno cambiante de hoy, debemos ser capaces de adaptarnos y cambiar junto con él para poder seguir haciendo las cosas que necesitamos. Esto se aplica tanto a nuestro trabajo, como al hogar y a los entornos de aprendizaje, y si necesitamos pasar todo nuestro tiempo averiguando cómo hacer nuestro trabajo, nunca lo lograremos.

Cuando se trata de aprendizaje en línea, es importante tener un sistema que sea fácil de usar pero que pueda utilizar toda la funcionalidad de un aula en persona de la vida real, como asignar tareas a los estudiantes, tener reuniones interactivas en vivo y probarlos en lo que tienen. aprendido. Además, por supuesto, también necesita una forma de calificar a sus estudiantes en función de su desempeño.

Google Classroom existe desde hace algún tiempo y siempre se está mejorando para que sea más fácil de usar y más capaz como herramienta de enseñanza y aprendizaje en línea. Con Classroom puede albergar varias clases con estudiantes específicos en cada clase y también tener los mismos estudiantes en varias clases. También puede preparar planes de lecciones, tareas, cuestionarios y otro material específico para cada una de sus clases o compartir el contenido entre algunas o todas sus clases.

El objetivo de este libro es ponerlo en funcionamiento con Google Classroom y mostrarle cómo crear sus clases, agregar estudiantes, distribuir sus materiales de aprendizaje y calificar el desempeño de sus estudiantes. También te mostraré cómo unirte y participar en una clase desde el punto de vista de un estudiante para que puedas ver cómo funciona cada lado. Verá que hay varias formas de realizar muchas de las tareas típicas que realizará, de modo que podrá encontrar la forma que funcione mejor para usted, o utilizar varios métodos.

Es muy probable que la forma en que utilice Google Classroom difiera de la forma en que lo utilizan otros profesores o estudiantes, por lo que es una buena idea conocer los entresijos de cómo funciona para que pueda realizar su trabajo sin importar dónde se encuentre dentro de la aplicación. . Una vez que aprendas Classroom, verás que no es tan difícil como podría parecer al principio. Entonces, en esa nota, ¡comencemos el proceso de aprendizaje!

Figure 7.7

Text Substitution
We all know that typing the same thing over and over again is no fun, especially if it's a hard to spell word, phrase, website address etc. Fortunately, there is a way to cut down on this tedious typing using the text substitution feature and you can get to it from the *Tools* menu by clicking on *Preferences*.

Docs has some built in text substitutions that you can use, or should I say will be used for you if you type in a certain word or character. If you look at figure 7.8 you can see that Docs will replace (c) with © automatically for you and also replace -> with an actual arrow character. If you don't want any of these built in substitutions to be made for you then you can simply uncheck the box next to it.

You might have noticed that I have added my own text substitution to the list at the top. So when I type in *oct*, Docs will substitute my website name *onlinecomptuertips.com* instead so I don't have to type out the entire address each time.

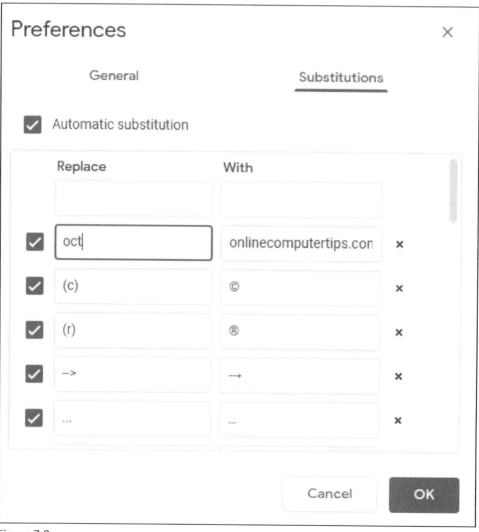

Figure 7.8

You can more of these to the list and each time you add one, Docs will create a blank area at the top of the list for the next one.

When using text substitutions, make sure you don't use a commonly used word for your substitution such as the word *work* to represent your company name because every time you type in the word work it will replace it with your company name and you most likely don't want that to happen.

Drag and Drop Text

When you are working on your documents you most likely end up changing things around such as rewording a sentence or deleting some text that just didn't fit the idea you were trying to convey.

If you find that you have some text such as an entire paragraph that needs to be somewhere else in your document then you can simply highlight the text you want to move and drag it where you would like it to go.

BEFORE

There are also folders within this classroom folder that are automatically created by Classroom as needed to organize certain files such as the responses to my Biography form assignment that were turned in by my students.

If you would like to see your Drive files for a certain class without having to go through the process of creating an assignment then you can go to the Classwork tab of that class and then click on *Class Drive folder* or click the folder icon on your class card.

You can also go to your Google Apps next to your profile picture and click on the Drive icon to open the Google Drive folders for your account which will show you all of your files and folders.

From here I can do things such as download my files to my hard drive, upload new files to my Google Drive or delete files I don't need anymore. I will be going into more detail on Google Drive in Chapter 6.

AFTER

There are also folders within this classroom folder that are automatically created by Classroom as needed to organize certain files such as the responses to my Biography form assignment that were turned in by my students.

From here I can do things such as download my files to my hard drive, upload new files to my Google Drive or delete files I don't need anymore. I will be going into more detail on Google Drive in Chapter 6.

If you would like to see your Drive files for a certain class without having to go through the process of creating an assignment then you can go to the Classwork tab of that class and then click on *Class Drive folder* or click the folder icon on your class card.

You can also go to your Google Apps next to your profile picture and click on the Drive icon to open the Google Drive folders for your account which will show you all of your files and folders.

Figure 7.9

I can't really show you the process in writing but what I would do is make a copy of a document that you can play around with and see if you can make this work for yourself.

Keyboard Shortcuts

If you have ever used Ctrl-C to copy or Ctrl-V to paste (Command-C and Command-v on a Mac), then you have used what is known as a keyboard shortcut. Keyboard shortcuts were designed to give you a way to complete commonly used tasks without having to use your mouse or click on any menu items or toolbar icons.

Docs will use the same keyboard shortcuts such as copy, paste, print, make text bold and so on that your operating system uses for other programs. If you would like to see what keyboard shortcuts are available for you to use within Docs then click on the *Help* menu and then on *Keyboard shortcuts* to see a listing.

Once you are there you can view the keyboard shortcuts by category or search for a particular shortcut from the search box.

Keyboard shortcuts	Q Search keyboard shortcuts	✕
Text formatting	**Text formatting**	
Paragraph formatting	Bold	Ctrl+B
	Italic	Ctrl+I
With objects	Underline	Ctrl+U
Editing	Strikethrough	Alt+Shift+5
Navigation	Superscript	Ctrl+.
Menus	Subscript	Ctrl+,
Comments	Clear formatting	Ctrl+\ or Ctrl+Space
	Paragraph formatting	
	Apply 'Normal text'	Ctrl+Alt+0 or Ctrl+Alt+Num-0
	Apply 'Heading 1'	Ctrl+Alt+1 or Ctrl+Alt+Num-1
	Apply 'Heading 2'	Ctrl+Alt+2 or Ctrl+Alt+Num-2
View all in help center	Apply 'Heading 3'	Ctrl+Alt+3 or Ctrl+Alt+Num-3

Figure 7.10

Add-ons

Add-ons are apps that you can install within Docs to improve its functionality or add additional features. There are many other software developers that create add-ons that you can use for free (for the most part). These add-ons are easy to install and how you use them will vary on the type of add-on you are trying out. The process for installing add-ons will vary and where you go to get them will vary as well since you won't find them all in one place. One place you can go to find may add-ons is the *Google Workspace Marketplace* located at: https://workspace.google.com/marketplace/

From there you can click on the link on the left that says *Works with Docs* and see if you can find anything that looks interesting to you. You can also search the apps from the search box at the top of the screen.

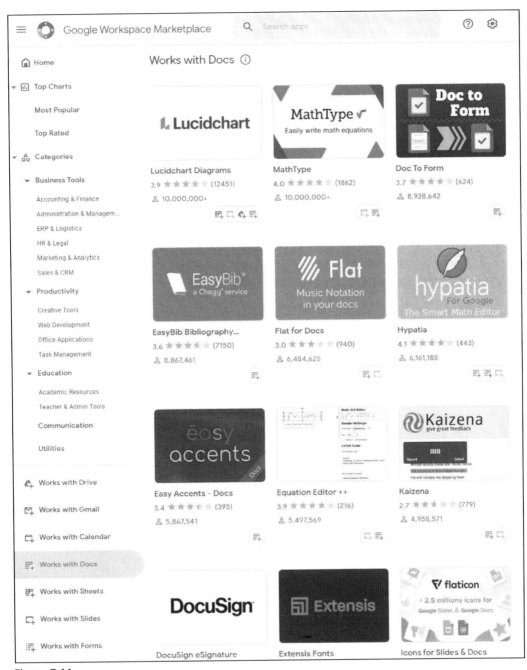

Figure 7.11

For my example I will be installing an add-on that lets you configure custom paper sizes in Docs since Docs is kind of limited as to what sizes you have to choose from. This add-on is called *Page Sizer* and once I go to their website all I need to do is click on the Install button.

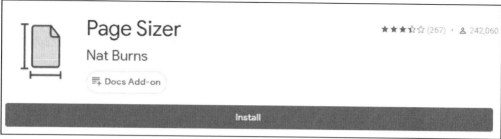

Figure 7.12

It will then tell me that I need to give the app permission to install by clicking on *Continue*.

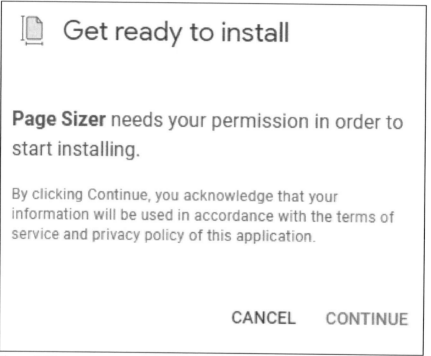

Figure 7.13

I will then be asked which account I want to use to install this app for. If you only have one Google account then it might not ask you this and just continue on. Most apps are account specific so if you install it while logged into one account then it won't be used for another Google account once you log in with that one.

I will then be told what access the add-on will need to my account in order for it to work so if something doesn't look right, don't install the add-on. I agree with the permissions the add-on needs so I will click on the *Allow* button.

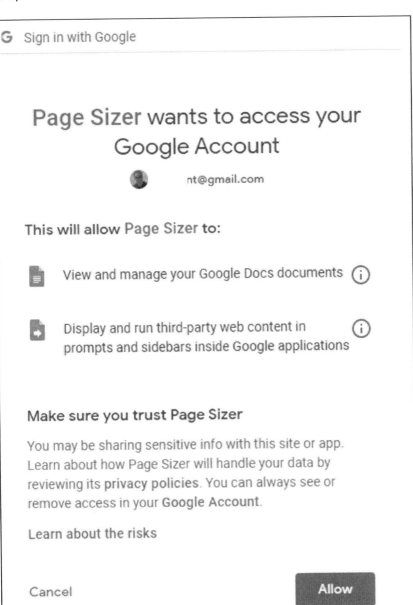

Figure 7.14

Finally, Page Resizer tells me that where to find the add-on and the installation is complete.

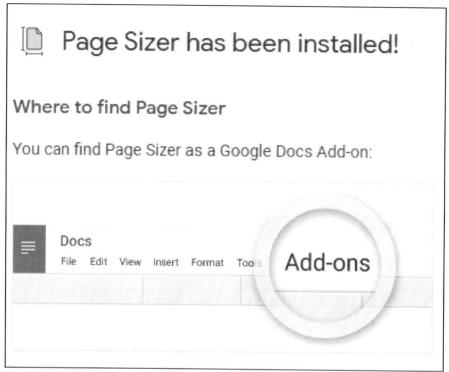

Figure 7.15

Now when I go back to Docs I can go to the Add-ons menu item and see my new Page Sizer add-on and start using it.

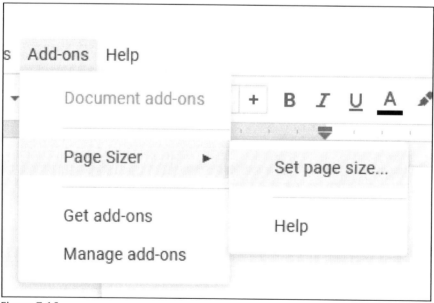

Figure 7.16

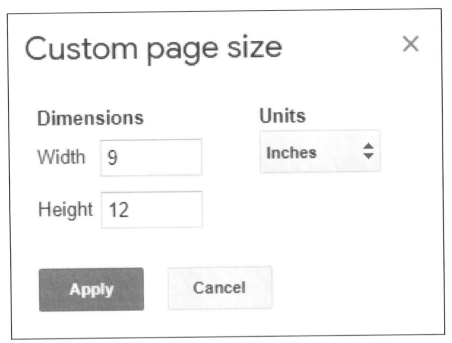

Figure 7.17

If you want to remove an add-on, go back to the Add-ons menu and then choose *Manage add-ons*. You will then be shown a list of all your installed add-ons and can uninstall them from there.

Comparing Documents

If you come across a situation where you find another copy of the same document and want to find out the difference between the two then you can run a comparison between them to find out.

To run the comparison, open one of the documents and then go to the *Tools* menu and then click on *Compare documents*. Then you will be asked to select the other file you want to compare from your Drive. In the section for *Attribute differences to*, you can enter the name of someone who will be listed as the author of the suggested edits in the comparison output file. I will change mine to Todd Simms and choose the file I wish to compare to my original document. If you want the comparison to show comments as well then check the box that says Include comments from the selected document.

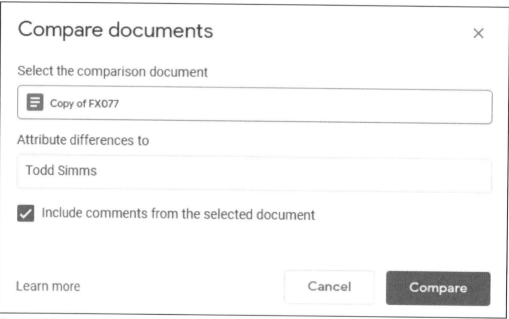

Figure 7.18

Compare documents   ✕

Select the comparison document

📄 Copy of FX077

Attribute differences to

Todd Simms

☑ Include comments from the selected document

Learn more   Cancel   **Compare**

Figure 7.19

Now that I have my selections the way I want I will click on the *Compare* button to start the process. When the process is complete all I need to do is click on the *Open* button.

Figure 7.20

Now I am shown all of the differences between my original file and the one I compared it to. As I scroll down the pages I can see exactly was these differences are.

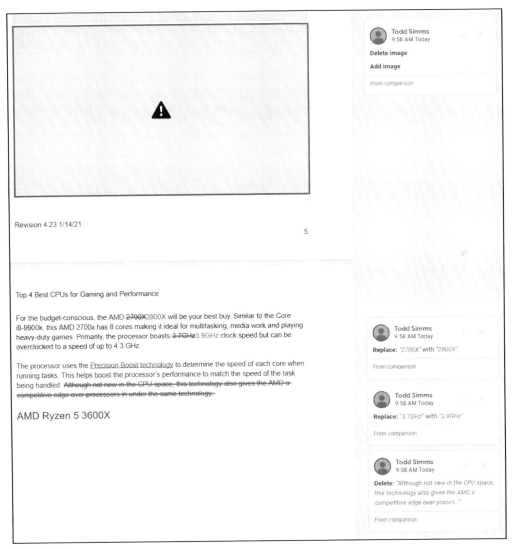

Figure 7.21

The comparison results will be saved in a new document called Comparison (document name) so you can go back to it and see the differences without having to run the comparison again. If you make additional changes to your document then you will have to run the comparison again to have it updated into a new comparison document.

Keep Notepad

Another useful Google App that you might want to consider using is called Keep. This app can be used to do things such as take notes, set reminders, create to-do lists, store photos and so on. You can also use Keep to collaborate with other people just like you do with Docs.

If you look over at the right side of the Docs window under your profile icon you will see a yellow lightbulb icon. This is a shortcut to the Keep notepad that will allow you to access your Keep notes from within Google Docs. You can also access Keep directly from the Keep website or by opening it via the icon under the Google Waffle where you have your Docs icon.

If you are a Keep user then you will see your notes when you click on this Keep shortcut as seen in figure 7.22. If you would like to use any of your notes in your document, all you need to do is drag it from your notes into you're the document itself.

Figure 7.22

This process also works the other way so if you have something in your document that you would like to save into your Keep notes then all you need to do is select that text or image etc., right click on it and choose *Save to Keep*.

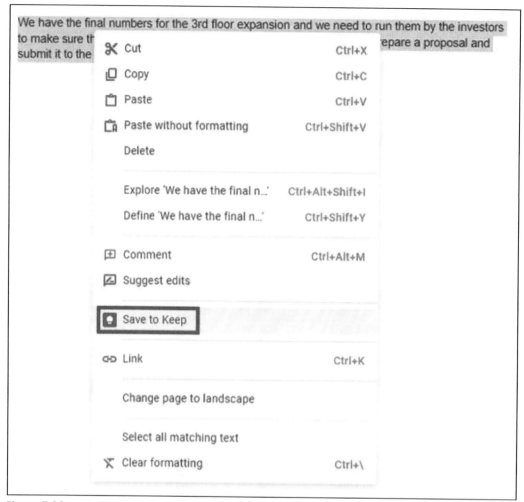

Figure 7.23

Then your item will show up in your Keep notes at the top of the list as seen in figure 7.24. And when you go to the Keep app itself, the item you added to your notes will show up there as well.

You can also click on *Take a note* in the notepad section to add a new note right from within Docs.

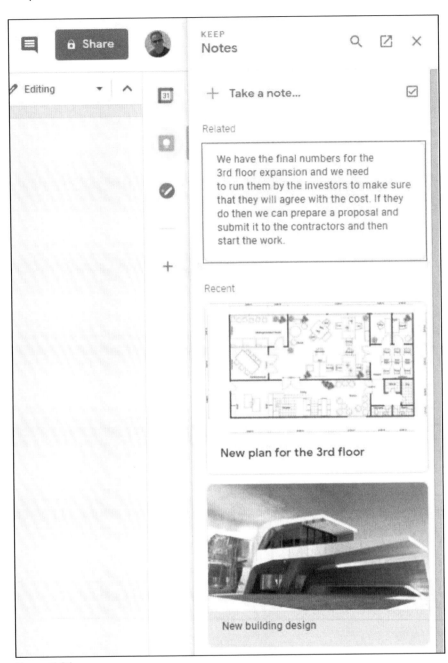

Figure 7.24

Tasks

Underneath the Keep icon you will see another item called Tasks that you can use to add items such as reminders and appointments to help you keep track of your schedule.

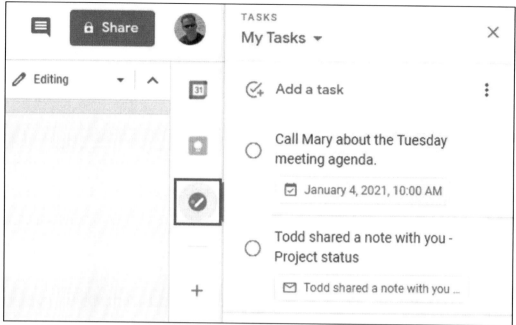

Figure 7.25

Then items with dates attached will be saved to your Google Calendar to help you stay on track... assuming you use the Google Calendar.

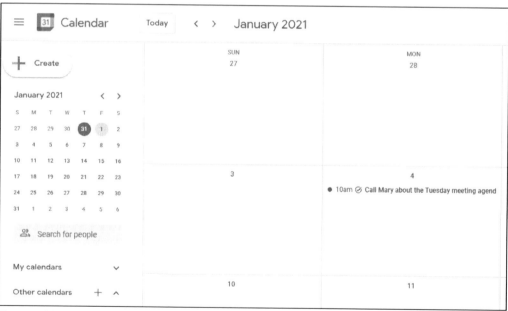

Figure 7.26

When you complete a task, you can then mark it as complete, so you know that you are finished with it.

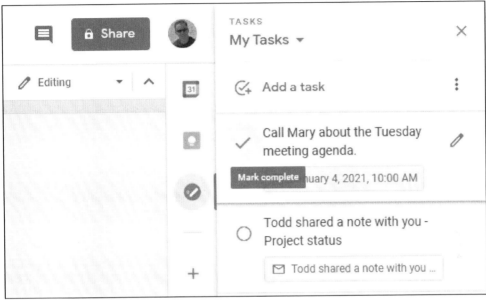

Figure 7.27

Adjusting Shared Document Links

As you know, you can share a document via a link and also adjust the permissions for that shared link so the people who use the link can either view or edit your document.

There is also a quick way you can use to adjust the link settings on the fly without having to generate a new link just by changing the last part of the link itself.

For example here is a link to a document that gives the recipient editor access only. Notice how it says **edit** at the end of the link.

https://docs.google.com/document/d/1o-trTFhXyPrYuVrH1jHFshb1zBnh9RN3MUR0Fi-UOUM/**edit**

If I were to change that link to say **/preview** at the end and send it to someone then they would only be able to view the document and would not have any tools available for them to even try to edit it.

https://docs.google.com/document/d/1o-
trTFhXyPrYuVrH1jHFshb1zBnh9RN3MUR0Fi-UOUM/**preview**

You can even add **/copy** to the end of the link so that when the person clicks on the link they will be asked if they want to make a copy of your document so they can work on their own rather than make changes to yours.

https://docs.google.com/document/d/1o-
trTFhXyPrYuVrH1jHFshb1zBnh9RN3MUR0Fi-UOUM/**copy**

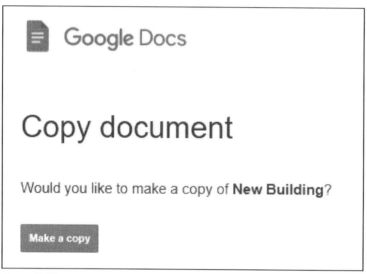

Figure 7.28

Opening PDF Files in Docs

When you click on a PDF file stored in your Drive or from your computer, Docs might try and open it within your web browser assuming you have the right browser plugin to view PDF files. If that's the case then you can click on *Open with Google Docs* to have the file open with Docs itself.

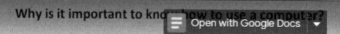

Why is it important to know how to use a computer?

Computers are everywhere and everyone is using them! Computers are in our cars, our kitchens, our stores and in our workplaces. They are used to communicate, to play, and to make everyday tasks easier. Using a computer and the Internet will help you to keep in touch with friends and family.

Figure 7.29

Once the file has been opened Docs, you will then be able to edit it and save it as your own document assuming the original PDF was scanned in using OCR (Optical Character Recognition) which is a technology that can scan a paper document and read the words and convert them to text. If the original file was converted to a PDF file on a computer then there shouldn't be a problem editing the text when you open it with Docs.

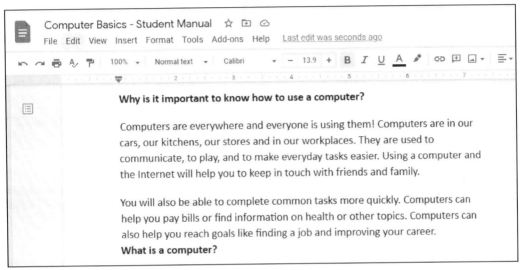

Figure 7.30

Linking to a Range in a Spreadsheet

As you might know by now, Google also has a spreadsheet app that they call *Google Sheets* and it's free to use as well if you even need to create and share data with other people.

Docs has the capability to link to a range of cells in one of your spreadsheets so you can share that data with other people who have access to your document. You will need to make sure that the people you will want to access this link also have permission to view your spreadsheet otherwise they will get an error message. If this happens they will be able to request access to your spreadsheet though.

To share a link to a range of cells in Sheets simply highlight the cells you would like to share, right click anywhere in the range and choose *Get link to this range*.

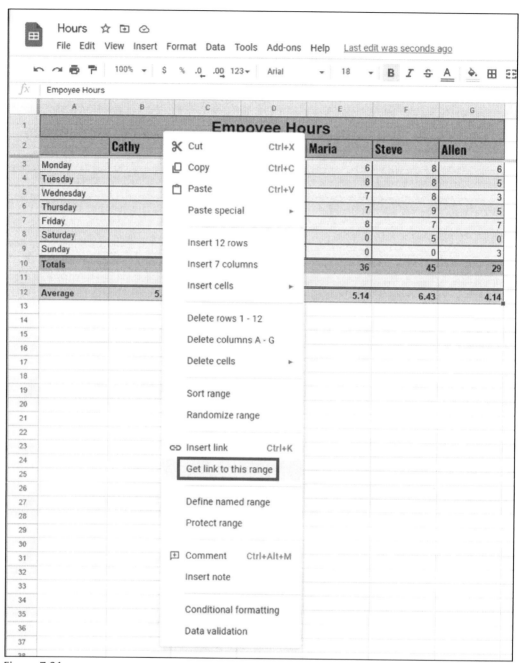

Figure 7.31

The link will automatically be created and copied for you so all you need to do is go into your document and paste the link. If you don't want to have a long ugly link in your document then you can add the link to a word, sentence or picture if you like as shown in figure 7.32.

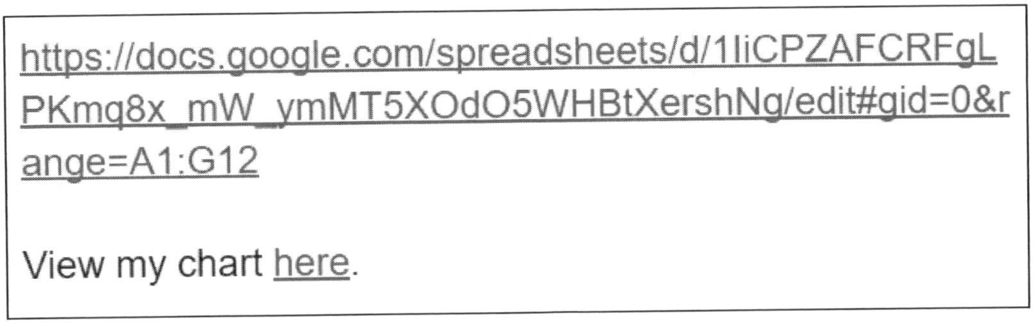

https://docs.google.com/spreadsheets/d/1liCPZAFCRFgL
PKmq8x_mW_ymMT5XOdO5WHBtXershNg/edit#gid=0&r
ange=A1:G12

View my chart here.

Figure 7.32

To add your link to a word or image etc., highlight the item and then choose the link option and then paste your spreadsheet link into the Link box. You can also change the text that is used from the Text box.

View my chart here

Text
here

Link
https://docs.google.com/spreadsheets/d/1liCF   Apply

Figure 7.33

Using Docs on Mobile Devices

Since many of us use our smartphones and tablets as much as, if not more than our desktop computers, it makes sense that we should be able to use Docs on these devices as well.

Google has a Docs app that you can download and install on your mobile device for free and then use to access all of your online documents. There is even a Drive app that you can install if you want to be able to see all of the files you have stored online. You can find the Docs app from the App Store (iPhones) or the Play Store (Android).

Once you install the app and log in with your Google account you will see you're the same files you see when you open them on your computer.

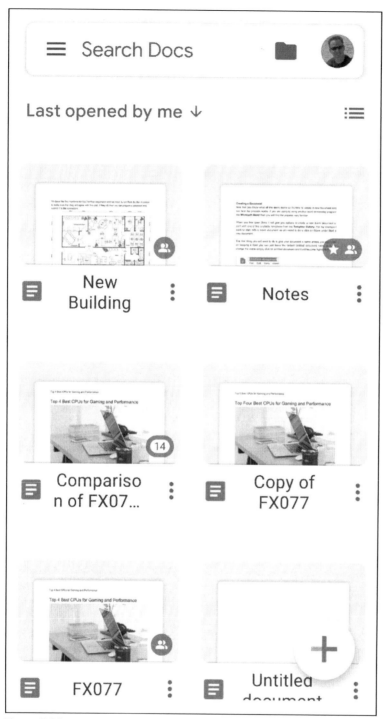

Figure 7.34

You can even change the view in the mobile app.

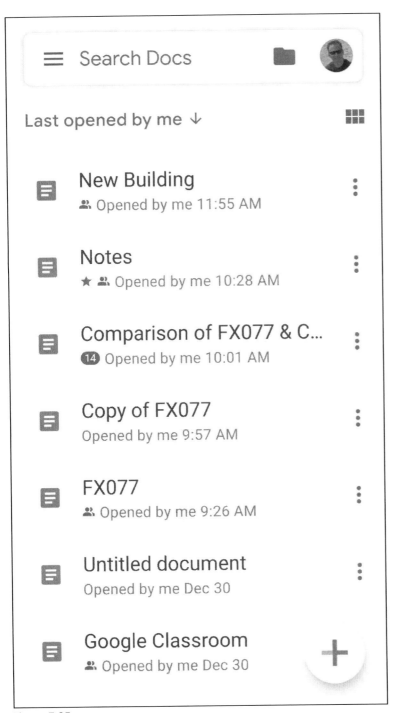

Figure 7.35

When you open a file you will be able to edit it just like you did on the computer but you will not see the same toolbar and menu icons so you might have to do a little searching to find the tools you need.

221

Figure 7.36

You should see three vertical lines stacked on top of each other at the top of the app (depending on your device) that will allow you to see the same categories as you do when on your computer.

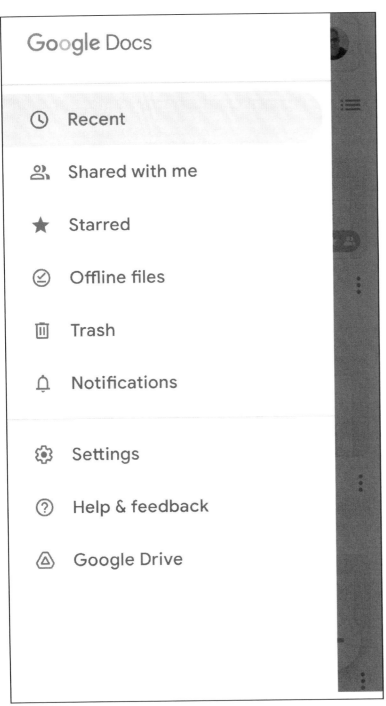

Figure 7.37

There should also be three vertical dots on top of each other that will open up some additional options.

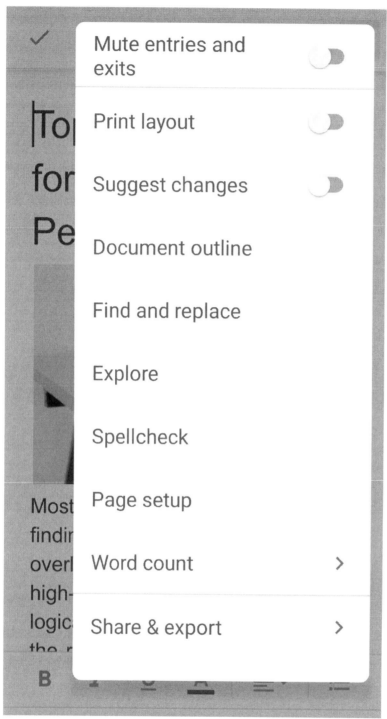

Figure 7.38

What's Next?

Now that you have read through this book and learned how Google Docs works and what you can do with the application, you might be wondering what you should do next. Well, that depends on where you want to go. Are you happy with what you have learned, or do you want to further your knowledge of the available Google apps such as Sheets and Slides and become a Google expert?

If you do want to expand your knowledge and computers in general, then you can look for some more advanced books on basic computers or focus on a specific technology such as Windows, Google Apps or Microsoft Office, if that's the path you choose to follow. Focus on mastering the basics, and then apply what you have learned when going to more advanced material.

There are many great video resources as well, such as Pluralsight or CBT Nuggets, which offer online subscriptions to training videos of every type imaginable. YouTube is also a great source for instructional videos if you know what to search for.

If you are content in being a proficient Docs user that knows more than your coworkers and friends then just keep on practicing what you have learned. Don't be afraid to poke around with some of the settings and tools that you normally don't use and see if you can figure out what they do without having to research it since learning by doing is the most effective method to gain new skills.

Thanks for reading **Google Docs Made Easy**. You can also check out the other books in the Made Easy series for additional computer related information and training. You can get more information on my other books on my Computers Made Easy Book Series website.

https://www.madeeasybookseries.com/

You should also check out my computer tips website, as well as follow it on Facebook to find more information on all kinds of computer topics.

www.onlinecomputertips.com
https://www.facebook.com/OnlineComputerTips/

About the Author

James Bernstein has been working with various companies in the IT field for over 20 years, managing technologies such as SAN and NAS storage, VMware, backups, Windows Servers, Active Directory, DNS, DHCP, Networking, Microsoft Office, Photoshop, Premiere, Exchange, and more.

He has obtained certifications from Microsoft, VMware, CompTIA, ShoreTel, and SNIA, and continues to strive to learn new technologies to further his knowledge on a variety of subjects.

He is also the founder of the website onlinecomputertips.com, which offers its readers valuable information on topics such as Windows, networking, hardware, software, and troubleshooting. James writes much of the content himself and adds new content on a regular basis. The site was started in 2005 and is still going strong today.

Printed in Great Britain
by Amazon

59370058R00129